English Premier League Academy Training Sessions

by
Rob Gale

Published by
WORLD CLASS COACHING

First published January, 2005 by
WORLD CLASS COACHING 15004 Buena Vista Drive, Leawood, KS 66224 (913) 402-0030

ISBN 0-9746723-3-5

Author - Rob Gale
Edited by Mike Saif

Front Cover - Designed by Babcock Illustration & Design. Photographs provided by Kidz-N-Sports Photography

Published by
WORLD CLASS COACHING

<u>*Acknowledgements*</u>

Express thanks to John Peacock for sharing material, wisdom and knowledge in compiling these drills. Thanks also to the Score UK coaching staff, both past and present. Also, thanks to Mick Gale for without whom Score UK Soccer would cease to exist so prosperously, and many of us would be bereft of enthusiasm for the game of Football. Finally, thanks to all the Gale family, especially, Erin for helping me become the player, coach and person I am today. Enjoy the book.

Rob Gale

English Premier League Academy Training Sessions

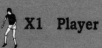 **X1   Player**

 **Path of Player**

Path of Ball

 Path of Dribble

 Target Area

<u>GLOSSARY OF TERMS</u>

ACTIVE DEFENDING – NORMAL TACKLING DEFENDING

CONDITION – PLACE A RESTRICTION ON

CONTROLLING SURFACE – PART OF BODY USED TO CONTROL BALL

DROP KICK – HALF VOLLEY FROM THE HANDS USED BY GOALIES

DUMMY – FAKE OR MOVE

FLANK – WING OR WIDE AREA OF FIELD

FOOTBALL = SOCCER

GIVE AND GO'S – ONE TWO – OR EXCHANGE OF PASSES

PASSIVE DEFENDING – CAN NOT TACKLE OPPONENT

SCRIMMAGE – MATCH OR GAME

TACKLE – CHALLENGE FOR THE BALL

THE READY POSITION – GOALKEEPERS STARTING POSITION – HANDS BY SIDE

VOLLEY – TO STRIKE THE BALL WHILST IT IS IN THE AIR

Warm Ups

The importance of warming up
- All athletes need to warm up before participating in practices and games
- Warm ups can be fun
- They should always be progressive
- They can be done with or without the ball

1st Phase of a warm up
- Light exercises that increase blood supply to the muscles
- Approximately 5-8 minutes
- Then introduce some stretching – larger muscles first
- Hold each stretch for 10-15 secs. Then progress to Phase Two

2nd Phase of a warm up
- Increase tempo and introduce turns, jumps – a variety of aerobic movements involving the joints
- Introduce stretches for 15-20 secs for each muscle

3rd Phase of a warm up
- Move into more explosive activities – increase space and distance for activities
- Introduce the theme of your coaching session to the warm up in basic form
- Stretches to finish should last 20 –25 secs.

Considerations
- Players should have stretched lower and upper body fully after warm up
- The warm up should last at least 30 minutes to get the athletes ready
- The stretches allow players recovery time to regulate their breathing
- Allow the players to hydrate with fluids – this will maintain their efficiency levels

Warm Ups

Fast Footwork exercises – 20 minutes
Organization: 48 markers in two lines 5 ft apart – space between cones 3 ft
1st Exercise: X jogs forward diagonally and zig zags all the way through markers to the end
X ^
^ ^

2nd Exercise: X side steps right around 1st marker then left around next etc. all the way to the end
X ^
^ ^

3rd Exercise : X runs forward then back on toes etc. right through markers
X ^
^ ^

4th Exercise : X starts facing outwards – high knees over all markers side ways on – on the way back facing markers just covered side step over and in between markers back to start
X ^
^ ^

Fast Footwork exercises – Increased Tempo – 20 minutes
Organization: 48 markers in two parallel lines 10 ft apart – space between cones 5 ft
1st Exercise: X runs forward to 1st cone – side -steps to cone on same side – back pedals to parallel cone behind – side-steps to next cone on that side, then repeats sequence all the way through cones
X ^
^ ^

2nd Exercise: 2 players at a time start on opposite sides, players run diagonally forward and zig zag all the way until the end, competitive, fun race and players have to avoid colliding
X ^
X ^

3rd Exercise: Two players again on opposite sides – run straight forward – jump and bounce off chests – back pedal to same marker, then side-step to next marker – run forward meet chests etc.
X ^
X ^

4th Exercise: Players perform 2nd Exercise again but as they cross paths now they use each other to spin off using their upper body – twist and keep running – meet in center each time
X ^
X ^

For all combinations of footwork drills players should lightly jog back after each completion – size of group ensures recovery period for each player will be sufficient – intersperse stretches as a group. Earliest Exercises should be lighter speeds with emphasis on small steps rather than dynamic Running. Increase tempo in latter stages and feel free to introduce a ball for all accommodating exercises.

Organization	Diagram

LADDERS

Players are paired up and numbered. Players face each other, sitting down toe to toe. Players should spread their legs as wide as possible and just be able to touch toes with players sitting next to them. When A players number is called they race against partner in and out of everyone's legs up around top marker and down the side of opposing team and around bottom marker before stepping back in and out teams legs until they sit back in position. The first player sitting down gets a point for their team.

Progression

After a while call more than one number at a time and the team with the most points wins.

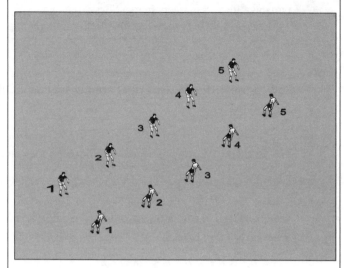

GALEY SAYS

All the players have a ball in 20 x 20-yard grid. The players are instructed to do skills by the coach i.e. Coach Galey. If the coach says "Galey Says" then the players have to do it. If coach does not say "Galey Says" first, then the players should not perform the skill. If they do, give them a light, fun punishment: juggles, toe taps or Australian push-ups etc.

Good Skills to Use

Dribbling Techniques, turns, juggling working from feet to head, flicking the ball up skills etc.

Key Factor

Coach should have a ball and demonstrate as much as possible – it helps to get players caught out.

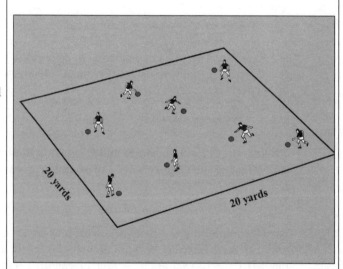

Warm Ups

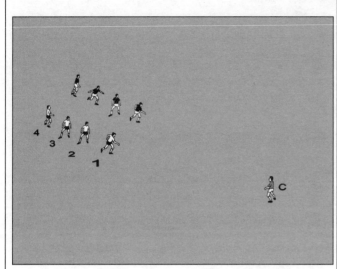

Organization
Coach (C) stands 15-yards away from the players who are standing side by side in pairs facing the coach. When the coach shouts "Go", number ones have to perform five of a set exercise, then sprint to the coach. The coach has his hands out and the player who slaps the coaches hand first scores a point for their team.

Work through each pairing for each exercise. The players should jog lightly back to end of line after each round. The team with the most points wins.

Exercises to Use:
* Press Ups – Push Ups
* Burpees
* Knee tucks to chest
* Sit Ups
* Bear Crawls
* Headers
* Star Jumps – Jumping Jacks
* Crab walks
* Forward Rolls
* Squat thrusts

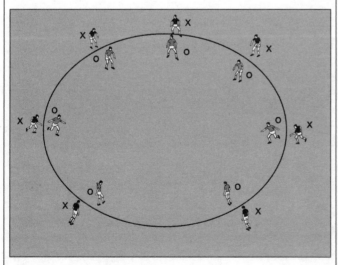

Organization
Partner up players. One player stands just inside the circle the other just behind them with a ball. O's have to pick X's up in piggy-back position. When coach shouts go, X's jump off back dribble ball clockwise around the outside of the circle and then control the ball before jumping back on partners back, shouting "Yeeha Grandma". Last player on partners back has to do fun task

Progression
Rotate so partners play and then make each round more complicated – i.e. players jump off then crawl through partners legs then dribble or players jump off, leap frog, then crawl through legs, then dribble and then make them repeat task after the dribble for added madness

Warm Ups

Organization	Diagram

Organization

The players are paired up and spread themselves across a 40 x 40-yard area. The players lay next to their partners flat on their stomachs. One pairing start the game as a chaser X and they chase their partner O. O has to avoid being tagged by X (they can lay down next to any player on the field), whoever they lay next to, that persons partner is now being chased by X and they have to jump up quick, avoid being tagged and run to lay next to a new person, and so the drill continues. If O gets tagged they become the new chaser and try to get the person who tagged them until they lay down and pass on the chase.

Progression

Increase to two chasers.

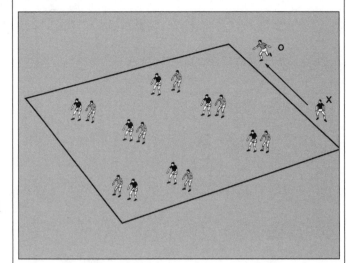

TOUCH AND MOVE

Divide the group into threes and line up as shown with about 3 ft between players in each group. A1 and A3's have a ball in their hands. A1 throws ball into A2 who side foot volleys back to A1's hands – they must catch the ball. A2 overlaps A1 and runs to A3 to perform same skill. A2 has to perform five volleys which are caught by partners and then overlap to complete the drill. The last group to finish each time does a fun task. Each player take turns to be the middle player.

Progression(s)

Change the skill to thigh then volley, chest then volley, head then volley, chest then head, single headers, double headers.

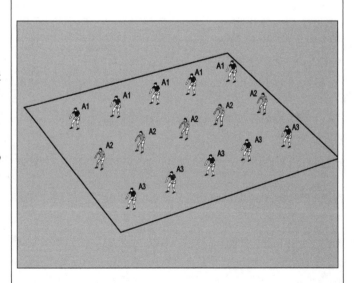

Diagram	Organization

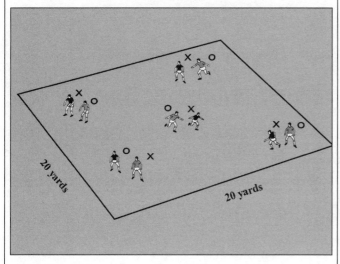

FOLLOW THE LEADER

The players are paired up. O has to run around the 20 x 20-yard grid area and X's have to mirror all of O's actions. Get players to side-step, jump for headers, touch ground, forward roll etc. Rotate so both players lead.

Progression(s)

Introduce a ball. The back player copies all tricks, turns etc. performed by leader with a ball. The front player has a ball and the back player follows without a ball, the front player has to lose the tail. Change so that the back player has the ball and front player jogs a little slower but tries to lose tail still. The front players have ball, but now they face the back player, run towards them with the ball and the back player must jockey in all the directions the lead player goes. Rotate.

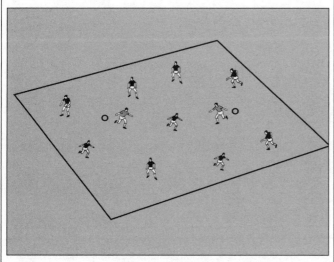

BIB TAG

All the players, except for two, tuck a bib/jersey into their shorts. The two players "O" have two minutes to try and pull the bib out of every one else's shorts. Rotate the chasers so that everyone has a turn. Reward points for anyone not getting caught. If players are caught they must stand to the side of the area. Remove all of the bibs and give two "O" players a ball each. The O's have two minutes to try and hit all the X's below the waist with the ball.

Organization	Diagram

TEAM BUILDERS

Divide the squad up into even numbers, three's or fours per sub-group. The coach stands in the center of the group and shouts commands. The last group to perform commands successfully does a fun task/punishment.

Tasks if Coach Shouts:

- "Front": players drop down lay on stomachs – and jump up again.
- "Back": players drop down lay flat on backs and jump again.

Coach combines tasks i.e. front, back, front, or front, front, back, back and players must stand in between each task. Later on, get the players to link arms as they perform each command as a group. Purely for your own entertainment!

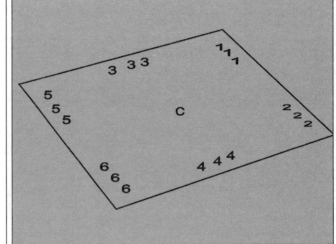

RELAYS

The group is divided into even numbers and each team stands in front of three markers all spaced five yards apart ahead of them. The teams perform relay races with different task in each one. The winning team gets to sit out the next race as an incentive.

Progression(s)

Alternate tasks in each race to without a ball then with a ball i.e. around first cone and back, slap next persons hand then dribble the ball around first cone and back, pass to the next player.

Bring in fun relays: piggy backs, wheelbarrow races, hopping, skipping.

Challenge players: volleys, ball control, touch drills with relay elements.

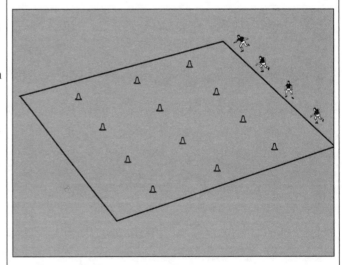

Warm Ups

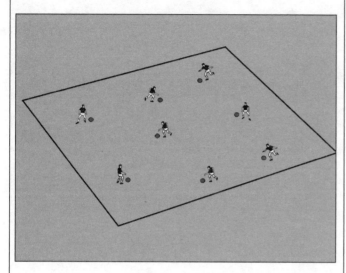

DRIBBLING WARM UP

Every player has ball in a 20 x 20-yard grid square. Players have to dribble the ball about and listen for coach to shout out a part of the body. When a body part gets shouted out the players have to react as quickly as possible and put that part of their body on the ball and hold it there until coach shouts a new command. The last player to put their body part on the ball has to do ten toe taps.

Progression(s)

Include a number command. When a coach shouts a number from 1 to 5 the players form groups of that number. If the coach shouts "10" every player has to get in a wheel barrow with a partner. If the coach shouts "20" everyone has to get a piggy back with a partner. The last groups have to do toe taps.

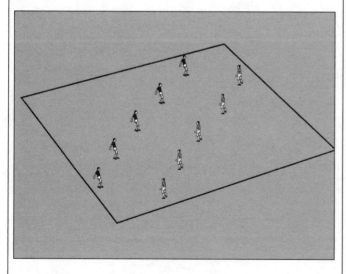

PARTNER WARS

Pair players up, as close to equal size and weight if possible. Players face each other ten feet apart. The players run into the middle of the area, bounce off each others chests and run backward to start position – repeat ten times.

Players face each other again ten feet apart, and run to the middle to link right arms and spin each other around and return to start positions – repeat ten times alternating spinning arms. 2nd player stands back to partner, hand on knees, head tucked in, ten feet away. The first player runs and leapfrogs partner, crawls back through their legs and returns to start position – repeat ten times.

Progression(s)

Rotate partners after each round. The last team to complete, do fun task.

Organization	Diagram

PARTNER WARS Cont'd

Players are paired up. The players grip hands and begin to rotate each others arms backwards and forwards slowly. On the coaches whistle, rotate back and forth really fast for 30 seconds.

Progression(s)

The players grab each other by the shoulders and on the coaches whistle the players try to wrestle each player and unbalance them. The players then go into squat positions facing each other and on the coaches whistle, the players try to slap each others thighs and knock their partner over.

ALL THESE DRILLS ARE DESIGNED FOR FUN ONLY AND PLAYERS / COACHES SHOULD EXERT CAUTION TO AVOID INJURIES

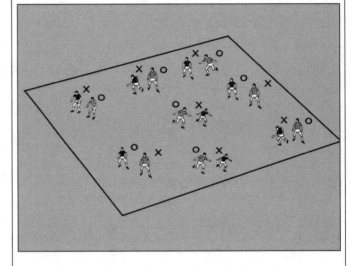

Passing

Push Pass
- Use Inside of the foot
- Non-kicking foot beside the ball
- Lock ankle - square to target
- Strike through center of the ball
- Follow through bringing knee up

Chip Pass
- Use knuckle of the big toe
- Non-kicking foot slightly behind the ball
- Approach from an angle
- Lean back into the strike
- Strike through bottom half of the ball
- Scuff the ground
- Bring knee up

Driven Pass
- Use laces instep
- Non-kicking foot beside the ball
- Approach from a slight angle
- Lean into the strike
- Strike through the center of the ball
- Keep knee, head and shoulder over the ball
- Follow through, pointing toe to target

Lofted Driven Pass
- Use knuckle of the big toe/laces
- Non-kicking foot slightly behind the ball
- Approach from an angle
- Lean back into the strike
- Strike through bottom half of the ball
- Follow through with toe pointing towards target
- Land on striking foot

Other Related Topics
- Curling the ball
- Body shape when receiving the ball and control
- Possession
- Movement off the ball
- Decision making - when to pass - what pass to use
- Productive passing - hurt the opposition - the split pass

Passing/Receiving

Organization	Diagram

Organization
X1 faces X2 only 3 ft away passing back and forth, working fast with a partner, counting how many passes they make.

Progression(s)
- Time limited to 45 seconds
- Use weaker foot only
- Players must control with one foot and pass with the other
- Limit to one touch
- Players have to beat their last score

Key Factors
- Use Inside of the foot
- Lock ankle square to the target
- Up on toes to receive a pass – move into line with the ball
- Communication – must call partners name

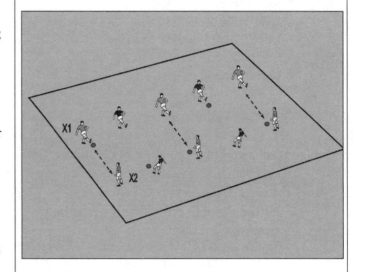

Organization
X1 passes to X2 through a 2ft gate placed in-between the players. X2 controls the ball and passes it back through the gate to X1. Players count how many passes go through the gate successfully in the time limit.

Progression(s)
- Condition passing foot
- Players have to control with the left and play with right foot and vice versa
- Reduce time
- Increase the distance
- If players miss a gate – there score returns to zero – keep count

Key Factors
- Technique as above
- Try to be quick but maintain accuracy
- Help partner with straight passes
- Be on your toes and meet the ball

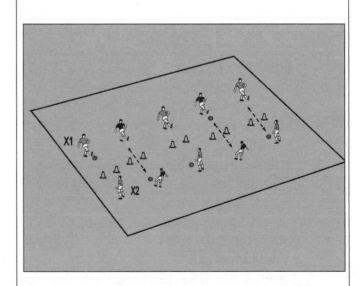

Passing/Receiving

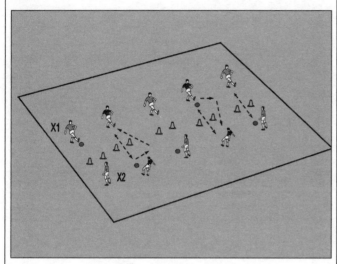

Organization

X1 passes ball to X2 through the gates. X2 takes the ball to the outside of the right foot and plays back down side of markers to X1. X1 keeps playing ball through the center cones. X2 uses alternate feet and plays back down alternate sides - reverse roles.

Progression(s)

Players then use the inside of the foot and take the ball across the body. Use disguise before making a move and playing the ball back to a partner. Place a time limit on the players – count how many tasks they can do in the allowed time.

Key Factors

- Communicate with your partner
- Use markers as a defender
- Take the ball out of the feet and make crisp passes back
- Throw a dummy/ disguise movement
- Quick change of feet after a dummy to make a quicker return pass
- Look up before passing

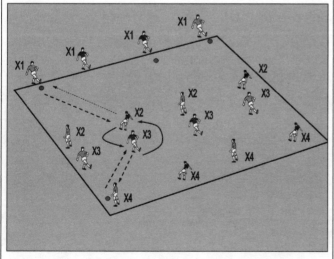

Organization

In groups of four, X1 and X2 face each other. X1 has a ball. X3 and X4 face each other, X4 has a ball. X1 and X4 pass to the middle X2 and X3 who return a pass, spin and face other end players – repeat.

Progression(s)

- All players rotate to be middle players and end players
- Limit the time
- Condition playing foot
- Throw balls in and get volleys back

Key Factors

- Accuracy a must to maintain speed of drill
- Communicate when you want the pass
- Central players use each other as defenders – roll or spin each other
- Up on toes – lock ankle
- Square, especially on volley

Organization: Support Ahead of the Ball

X1 has the ball in the center. X2 and X3 move into 45 degree
angles to create a triangle. X1 has a choice of pass to X2
or X3. Once X1 passes he makes a support run through the
middle to form new triangle.

Progression(s)

Player who receives ball makes the same choice and play
continues with each passer making support runs to form
new triangles. Condition the number of touches on the ball.
Condition the controlling and passing foot, - left only, right,
alternate.

Key Factors

Communication from all the players:
- Do you want to receive?
- Who are you passing to?
- Timing and weight of pass
- Body shape to receive pass
- Good 1st touch
- Quick support runs – see the ball as you run – shape

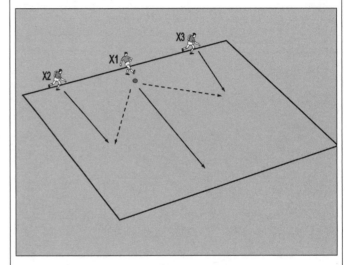

Organization: Blind Side Runs

X1 has the ball in the center. X1 plays the ball ahead for X2
to move onto and makes a blind side run on X2. X2 does the
same with X3 and X3 then does same with X1. Play up until
halfway line and return.

Progression(s)

- All the players should be on the move
- Condition to two touch
- Condition to one touch
- Increase the distance between the players from 5 ft to 10 ft
  for added endurance

Key Factors

- Passes should be in front of the next player
- Runs should be sharp and on blind side i.e. behind player
  you passed to
- Timing of the pass and runs are vital to the success of the
  drill, as are the quality of passes:
  – timing
  – distance
  – weight and accuracy

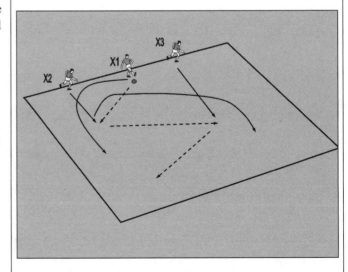

Diagram	Organization

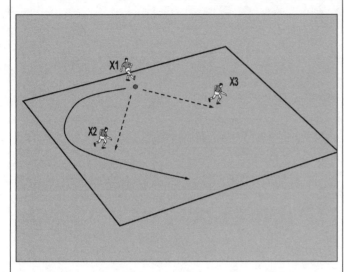

Organization: Overlaps

Combination of the last two practices. X1 has ball – players move ahead to create triangle as in first drill while X1 now makes a full overlap run after the pass to create a triangle again.

Progression(s)

- Condition the players touches on the ball
  - numbers and feet used
- Increase the distance for a driven pass and longer overlaps

Key Factors

- Always keep the body shape open for the next pass
- Always see the ball and the field – head up, looking around
- Communication between all the players should be constant

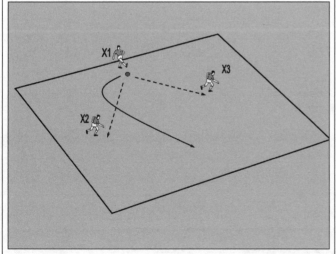

Organization: Under-laps

Exactly the same format as the previous drill. X1 starts with ball and plays pass but now makes a curved run inside of the receiver (an under lap).

Progression(s)

- Condition the players touches on the ball
  - numbers and feet used
- Increase the distance for a driven pass and longer runs off the ball

Key Factors

- End to use any of the four passing and movement combinations
- All the players should see the ball at all times and always be in a position to receive the next pass
- Players should know where they will make their next pass and be in a position to do this – in 1 touch

Passing Games

Organization: Ten Pin

Two teams of equal numbers. Each player has a ball. On 'GO' the first player tries to pass ball and knock down the cones. Players fetch the balls and join the end of their teams' line.

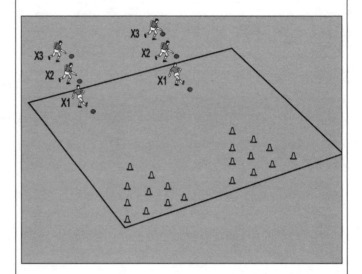

Progression(s)
- Teams continue to pass until one team knocks all the skittles down to win
- Condition the passing foot
- Make the cones wider apart
- Increase the distance

Key Factors
- Use the inside of the foot
- Lock the ankle square to the target
- Fetch the ball back quickly and get into position to shoot again – take it in turns
- Only one shooter at a time
- Can not shoot from close in

Organization: "Clean your Rooms"

Two teams of equal numbers. Every player has a ball. On 'go' all players pass ball into other teams 'room'. Players pass back and forth in time limit.

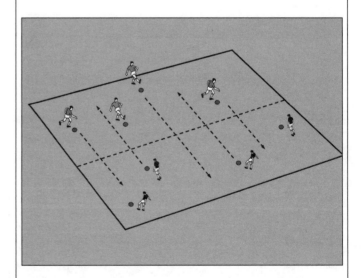

Progression(s)
- Balls must stay in room to count
- Teams with least balls in their room i.e. the tidiest room wins
- Reduce room size
- Condition passing foot
- Limit time of each game

Key Factors
- Balls must stay below waist height
- Inside of the foot passing only
- No hands allowed to control other teams passes or retrieve balls back to rooms

Passing Games

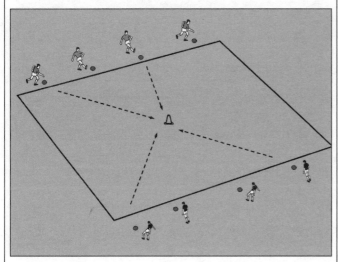

Organization: Pinball

Two teams of equal numbers. Everyone has a ball. The players have to pass their ball and hit a target (PINBALL) in the middle. The team who knocks the PINBALL over the other teams end line wins. Must shoot from behind own end line

Progression(s)

- Condition the passing foot
- Increase the distance away from opponents
- Bring in more pinball's
- No kicking the Pinball

Key Factors

- Side foot passes only
- Make sure as distance increases that the technique remains constant
- Fetch spare balls quickly and keep shooting at the pinball

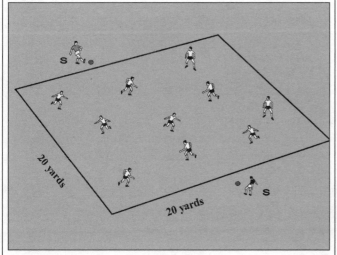

Organization

Two players are sharks (S) the rest are minnows. Sharks have a ball. Minnows must stay in 20 x 20-yard grid. Sharks have to hit all minnows below the waist with the ball.

Progression(s)

- Limit sharks time to two minutes to get all minnows
- Condition passing foot
- Once minnows are out you can let them become sharks – if the sharks struggle

Key Factors

- Passing must stay below the waist
- Supply of balls should be around the square to keep minnows moving
- Accuracy before power – hit don't hurt minnows
- Work hard for two minutes and get everyone out!!!

Passing/Possession

Organization: Pass to Induce a Move

Using 10 X 10-yard grids with three players to a grid in the
corners. X1 plays a ball to spare corner for X3 to meets that
ball at corner. X3 then plays a pass to the marker he left. X2
meets that pass at that marker. Continue the sequence.

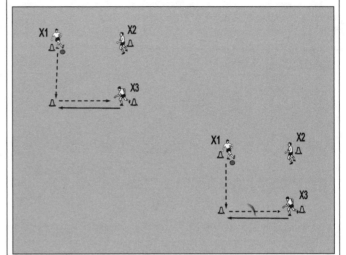

Progression(s)
- Limit the players to two touches
- Reverse the direction of the passing
- Limit the players to one touch if they are of a high standard

Key Factors
- Timing and weight of pass
- Verbal and Physical Communication - when to pass and
  where
- Body shape – Open up to play next pass early
- Sharp runs to keep the drill at a fast pace

Organization: Move to Induce a Pass

Using 10 X 10-yard grids, X2 starts with ball and chooses
pass to X1 or X3. The player who does not receive the ball
moves to provide a second option for the receiver – square
pass. Continue the sequence.

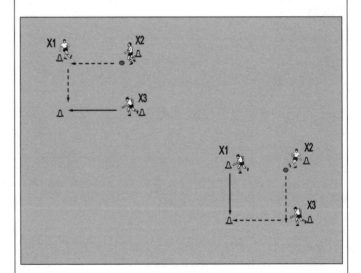

Progression(s)
- Limit the players touches
- Condition the touches to one with each foot for quicker
  play
- Reverse the passing direction

Key Factors
- Timing and weight of pass
- Verbal and physical communication - when to pass and
  where
- Body shape – Open up to play the next pass early
- Sharp early runs to keep the drill at a fast pace

Passing/Possession

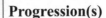

Organization: 3 v 1

Using 10 x 10-yard grids with three players in corners and one defender (D) in the middle. D holds pinny/bib. X's pass and move trying to keep the ball inside the square and away from D. If D wins ball losing X goes in middle and takes over the pinny/bib and becomes the new D.

Progression(s)

• Make the defender passive if struggling – then active
• Award a point for ten consecutive passes
• D stays in twice for a nutmeg
• Limit X's touches – 2 touch then 1

Key Factors

• Movement off the ball
• Quality of passing
• Communication
• Decision making:
  - Draw the defender then play a pass
  - Keep the ball moving – don't over play or get caught in possession
• Good body shape – 1st touch sets to pass quickly

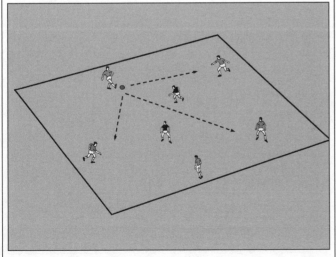

Organization: 5 v 2

Using a 20 x 20-yard grid. X's have to keep the ball away from D's. Same rules as above – whoever loses possession becomes a defender.

Progression(s)

• Limit X's touches
• Passive then active D's
• Reward ten passes and reward split passes

Key Factors

• Use and range of passes – bigger area – switch play
• Switch quickly from defender to attacker
• Look to split defenders – play between players
• Communication is KEY

Passing/Possession

Organization: Draw and Switch

Using 30 X 15-yard grid with two groups of three players in each end zone and defenders in middle. X1's must make five passes before switching ball to X2's. D1 allowed to win ball back after X's touch the ball. X2's receive driven pass and repeat to X1 after they make five passes.

Progression(s)

- Allow D's in the middle to try and intercept pass
- Limit X's touches
- X's that lose possession then become D's
- Reward every switched pass with points
- Allow two defenders to challenge X's in end zone

Key Factors

- Quick passing to get five passes
- Set up the switch
- Movement off the ball - good support angles
- good 1st touch on the switched possession
- communication between X's at opposite ends

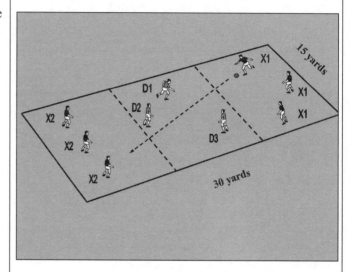

Organization: Switch and Support

Using 40 X 40-yard grid with players in groups of three. X1 plays one-two with X2 and then drives a ball to X3. X1 and X2 switch positions. X3 plays a one-two with X1 and drives to X2 - repeat sequence.

Progression(s)

- Condition controlling touches
- Condition driven pass to certain target heights i.e. - drive to chest, etc.
- Challenge players by merging groups so players can then pass to any X1, X2 or X3
- Reduce number of balls and add in defenders

Key Factors

- Short, short, long sequence - make angled pass to set switch pass.
- When merged, talk should be early and loud between all groups
- Drive, don't chip longer pass
- Make controlling touch a pass if possible

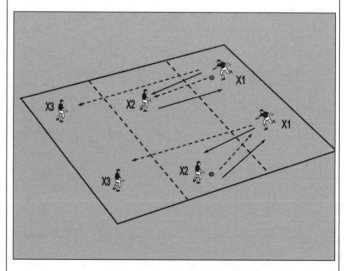

Passing/Possession

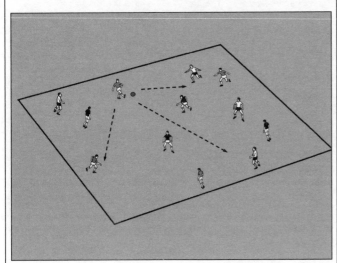

Organization - Three Team Keep Ball
Three equal teams play within a 40 X 40-yard grid. X's and O's try to keep possession away from D's. If a team loses possession, they become the defending team.

Progression(s)
- Reward ten consecutive passes
- Limit players touches
- Bring in a neutral target player - reward if they find target player with the ball whilst in possession

Key Factors
- Communication between two teams in possession
- Win ball back and switch from defensive mind set early
- Use the space - draw the player then switch
- Play between players - move off the ball

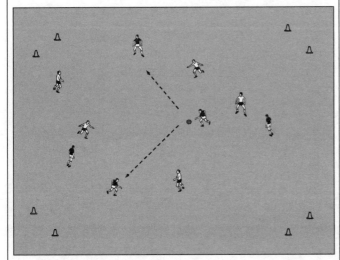

Organization - Four Corners Game
Two teams of equal numbers play within a 40 X 40-yard area - no out-lines just four corner goals. Teams attack other tams goals - in opposite corners.

Progression(s)
- No goalkeepers
- Play two or three touch
- reward bonus goal if they attack and score in opposite corners in the same move
- Introduce goalkeepers

Key Factors
- Be calm in possession
- Use the field
- Switch early and catch defenders unaware
- Keep possession - make the other team run
- Maintain a team shape - attack in small groups

Ball Control

- Be Up on toes ready to control ball at all times
- Judge height and pace of ball and get into line to control
- Select controlling surface early
- Offer controlling surface
- Be aware of position ready to make next move
- Take controlling surface away
- Make next play

Foot Control
- Do not trap under the foot
- Use laces or inside of the foot
- Control in front away from the body ready to play
- Play with opposite foot to increase speed of play

Thigh Control
- Make sure muscle is relaxed
- Stay in line with ball in case of miss-control
- Drop knee away to play from feet
- Try to control across your body and shield from opponent

Chest Control
- Arms out for balance and protection
- Lean back then drop chest away on touch
- Control with muscle of chest
- Take ball across the body to opposite foot or thigh

Head Control
- Take sting out of the ball
- Relax neck into shoulders
- Use forehead - parallel to the ground
- Try to control into stride

Other Related Topics
- Importance of the first touch
- Ball juggling
- Volleying
- Decision making - control is the means to an end - dribble, pass, shoot

Ball Control

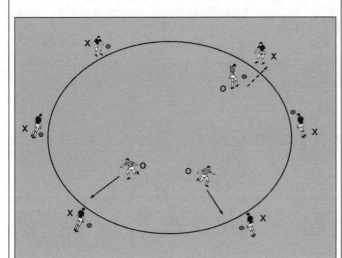

Organization

Two thirds of all players on outside of circle - one third inside. O's run to player on outside of circle who serve a ball in the air for O to control with feet. O controls, passes back and then overlaps X and repeats.

Progression(s)

- Rotate so all players go in the middle
- Condition controlling touches - control with one foot and pass with the other
- Players must volley 1st time back to outside
- Control with one foot - volley with the other
- Add a defender

Key Factors

- Quick runs into players, slow down on arrival
- Be up on toes, adjust to height and weight of serve
- Relax on controlling touch
- Control out of your stride and play back quickly
- Don't go round in a circle - overlap then move across circle - look up as you run

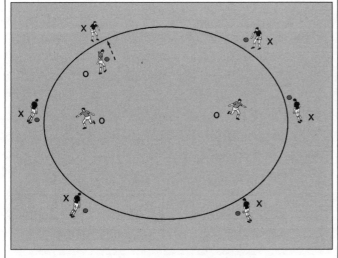

Organization - Thigh Control

Exactly the same setup as above. Players must now take controlling touch with thigh and play back to partners before overlapping and finding a new server. How many can a player do in a minute?

Progression(s)

- Rotate so all players go in the middle
- Condition controlling touches - control with one thigh and pass with the opposite foot
- Players must control with thigh then laces volley back to the outside
- Add a defender to pressure the first touch

Key Factors

- Offer thigh and as ball touches, drop away to land the ball at your feet
- Try to control across your body to play early
- As body tires during the minute, try to keep mind focused
- Thigh muscle stays relaxed to control each time

Ball Control

Organization - Chest Control

Same format as before. Players must take controlling touch with chest and play back to partners before overlapping and finding new server. How many can player do in a minute?

Progression(s)

Rotate all players through the middle
- Condition passing/volleying foot
- Chest then head back to partners – must attack ball at pace for this
- Bring in a defender to put pressure on one of the tasks - (passive at first)

Key Factors

When controlling with the chest, lean back and drop your chest away as you control. Get your arms out for balance and protection. Be aware of defenders positioning and your own space in which to control the ball. Use your body to shield and control into space.

Keep the work rate going.

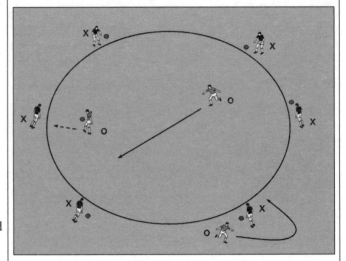

Organization - Head Control

Continue the format, resting the players for two minutes then working them for one. The players control with their head to feet, then play a pass, then progress to controlling with the head to a volleyed pass.

Progression(s)

- Controlled header straight back to the outside players
- Control with head then pass with a header
- Bring in passive defenders on controlling drills

Key Factors

- Approach slightly slower
- Tilt head back and relax the neck into the shoulders to control
- On headed passes, bullet the ball back to partners
- Replace overlaps on the outside with turns and spins at any time

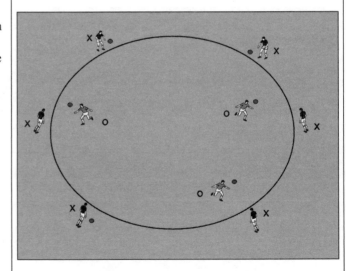

Ball Control

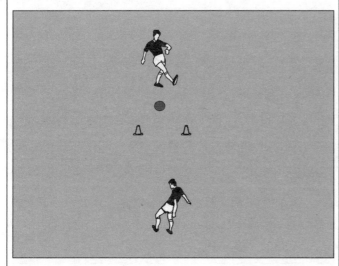

Organization
Working in pairs, ten feet apart. X1 serves the ball from his hands into X2 who controls the ball with his feet and passes in back through the gate. Repeat ten times and swap positions. Award a score out of 10 for passing through the gate.

Progression(s)
- First time volleys
- Thigh control - Pass, then thigh and volley
- Chest control - Pass, then chest and volley
- Head control - Pass, head then volley

Key Factors
- Vary the height and weight of the serve to test the partner
- Adjust quickly to serve and be in place for a soft touch
- Concentrate on firing pass or volley through the gate
- Always be on your toes and ready for the next serve in

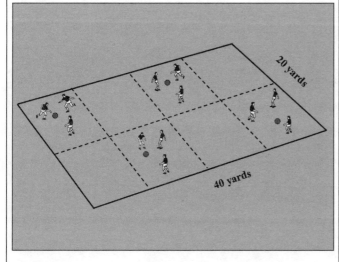

20 yards

40 yards

Organization
Divide the team into even groups and place in 10 x 10-yard areas with space clockwise between each group.. Players have to perform a task set by the coach and move into the next square. Repeat the task before moving again. The first team back to their starting grid wins.

Progression(s)
Set tasks like these:
- 20 one touch passes in the air
- 20 consecutive two touch juggles (alternating players each time, using feet only or using thighs only)
- 20 headers alternating players each header
- 10 double headers, alternating players each time

Key Factors
- Try to get the groups performing the correct techniques while racing each other
- Remain calm and take small touches
- Don't look at other groups' progress
- Run quickly between grids and set yourself before beginning again
- Make sure you compete the task properly be fore moving on

Ball Control

Organization

Exactly the same drill as previously in format. Now players have to catch the next group, if they do, they eliminate them from the game. If the players do not perform the task, then they must start again from zero.

Progression(s)

- Increase the number of grids and reduce the number of players to make the groups work harder in these elimination stages
- Make the tasks more complex, add runs or spins to test the players further between skills

Key Factors

- Players must focus their minds when fatigue sets in and touch starts to go
- Complete the skill with good technique, rather than rushing; that will move you on quicker than being frantic

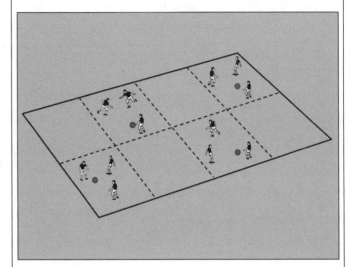

Organization

4 v 4 in a reduced sized area to encourage throw ins and corners etc. Players must score with a header or a volley.

Progression(s)

Restrict players to two touch finishes where they must control before shooting, then introduce one touch finishing.

Key Factors

- Keep the game at a high tempo, with lots of balls around the side for quick re-starts
- Encourage the players to play aerial balls

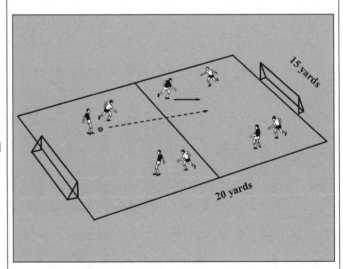

15 yards

20 yards

Ball Control

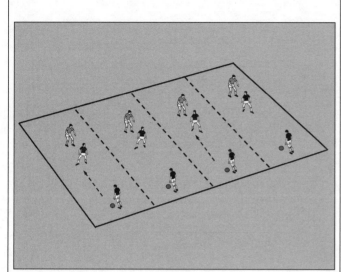

Organization
Three players per 20 X 10-foot grid. X1's have a ball and serve to X2's feet on X2's shout. X2 controls under slight pressure from X3 - tries to get half turn and then plays back to X1. Repeat 10 times

Progression(s)
- Rotate so all players control, serve and pressure
- Condition controlling touches - control with one foot and play with the other
- Vary height and pace of serve in
- After one round get servers to play in with feet

Key Factors
- Maximise your space to receive the ball
- Create space away from defender and demand service with verbal or physical communication
- Control sideways on - keep your body between defender and the ball
- Always look to turn defender but play back to X1 accurately

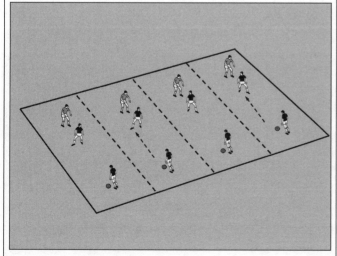

Organization - Thigh, Chest and Head
Exactly the same scenario as above but serves are aimed at thigh, chest and head. The players should rotate every position after each set of ten serves. If players are taking it easy, increase defenders privileges to full tackling.

Progression(s)
- Try to condition players to controlling to side: left thigh to right foot, left pectoral etc.
- Test players with variety of serves - looped, flat - hard, soft
- If players are of sufficient quality, allow chipped services

Key Factors
- Players must get used to feeling defender and pushing away to get space to control
- Always get sideways on if possible and try and roll defender
- Be aware of distance between you and server and you and defender
- Keep focus as legs and mind get heavy

Ball Control

Organization - Control and shoot

Exactly the same scenario as before - each group numbered with a server (s) - an attacker (a) and defender (d). Now players are encouraged to turn, attack and score. Players to keep count of number of successes - points for goals and defenders and saves.

Progression(s)

- All players to participate in each role
- Five shot attempts each then bring in a GK
- Allow servers to receive passes back and play through balls for attackers
- Join two groups together for two on two's

Key Factors

- Encourage players to practice same technique as before - now with an end result
- Composure in front of goal after control to beat defender
- Use server with pass back and spin defender
- Communication - when you want passes and where

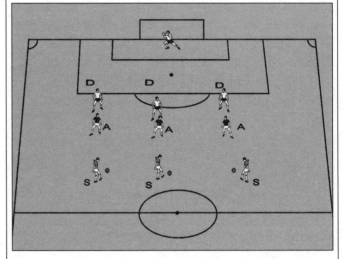

Organization

Two attackers (a) take turns in receiving serves from servers (s) 1-7 on outside of goal area. Players have to control and shoot to score past GK. Rotate all positions

Progression(s)

- Coach calls numbers for servers to play balls in
- Limit number of touches for attackers
- Bring in passive then active defenders
- Allow chipped serves

Key Factors

- Put into practice all the skills learned previously
- Choice of finish after control is vital
- Be aware of surroundings - GK's position, defender's position - your space and time

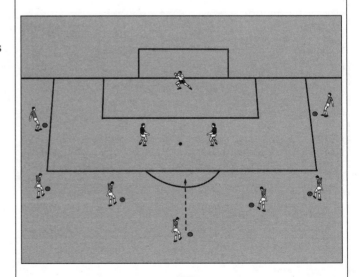

Juggling

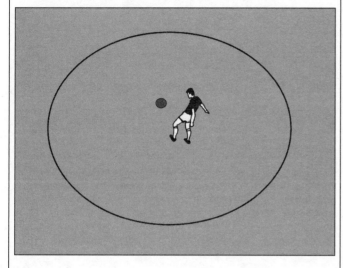

Individual Drills

- The player has a ten yard circle to work in. The player tries to perform six juggles with the feet only, the ball is allowed to bounce once in between each juggle
- The player then tries to juggle the ball six times without the ball bouncing
- The player tries to perform three juggles, allows the ball to bounce and then three more using knees or feet only
- The player tries to perform eight consecutive juggles with knees or feet without the ball bouncing
- The player tries to perform as many consecutive juggles as possible with any part of the body
- The player tries to perform as many juggles as possible incorporating as many body parts as possible

Pair Drills

The players have a fifteen yard circle for the drills:

- The players try to perform ten juggles passed between them with single touches. The ball is allowed to bounce in-between juggles
- The players try to perform three juggles each, then they pass to their partners, letting the ball bounce in-between. This is repeated three times with eighteen juggles total
- The players try the same exercises but without the ball bouncing
- The players try to perform the same exercise:
  - With feet only
  - With knees only
  - With head only
- The players juggle one touch back and forth without the ball hitting the ground
- The players have two touches each, but with a different body part each time
- Three touches, each with a different body part

Juggling

Group Drills

Using an even number of players, each in a 10 x 10-yard grid the players have to keep the ball in the air between them. On the coaches whistle the players transfer their ball to the next grid clockwise. Teams should attempt to receive the ball and continue to juggle. Award points for each juggle and see which team gets the most consecutive juggles.

Make Players Use:

- Feet only
- Knees and feet only
- Headers only
- One touch only
- Must take two touches per player
- Two and then three touches with different parts of the body each time

Key Factors for Juggling

- Do not panic at any time
- When working with a partner, try to give high looping service so that they have time to adjust
- Always try to beat your last score, do not compete with anyone but yourself
- Try flicking the ball up to start

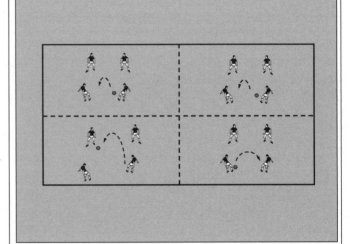

Juggling Games:
Football Volleyball/Football Tennis

Using the same dimensions of a volleyball or tennis court, play the same rules but players can not use their hands.. Condition the number of touches per player and per team in a rally.

Donkey

Using smaller groups, all the players outside of a circle. Player one serves the ball from his thigh into another player. Players must take two touches exactly and keep the juggle going. If the ball drops, the player who makes the mistake becomes the letter "D". Play continues until someone becomes a donkey.

Key Factors for Juggling

- Players should try and maintain balance at all times
- Players should relax controlling muscle
- Laces touches should bring the toe up and spin the ball backwards
- Knees touches stay below head height
- Try to use both feet alternatively or if using knees, use a marching style for greater balance and control
- Try to select best body part for the next touch as early as possible

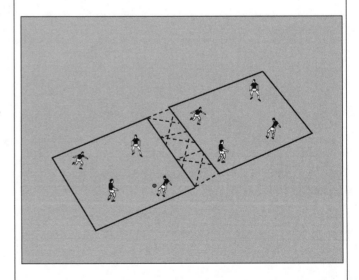

Volley's/Touch Drills

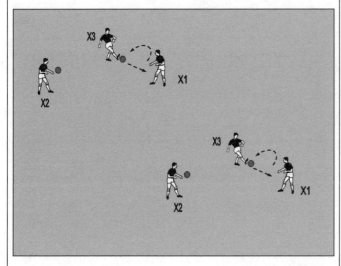

Organization - Sideways on Volleys
In groups of three, players form a triangle with X1 and X2 having a soccer ball. X1 throws ball to X3 who volleys right footed back into X1's hands. X2 throws to X3 who volleys left footed back into X2's hands.

Progression(s)
- All players take turns in each role
- Place time restriction on volleying player, i.e. 60 secs
- Keep count on number of volleys into hands
- Add a controlling touch - knee, chest etc

Key Factors
- Quality serves - don't let player rest
- Firm volley - up on toes
- Change sides quickly
- Good body shape - sideways on
- Relax on controlling touch

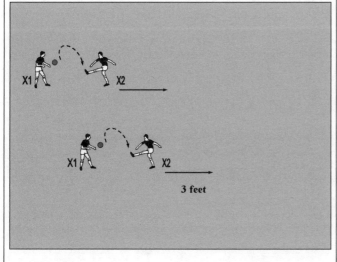

3 feet

Organization - Defending Volleys
Working in pairs players face each other 3 or 4 feet apart. X1 throws to X2 who volleys side foot back into X1's hands. X2 runs backwards three feet quickly. X1 follows X2 and keeps throwing. Repeat sequence.

Progression(s)
- Work half the length of the field
- Change places with partner and work back to the start
- Condition volleying foot - left then right
- Introduce controlling touch - Knee, chest, head - then volley etc

Key Factors
- Up on your toes - firm volleys with inside of foot
- Take quick steps back and set up for next volley
- Vary height and weight of serves
- Keep serves coming quick
- Relax on controlling touch and set for volley

Volley's/Touch Drills

Organization - Attacking Volleys

Working in pairs players face each other 3 or 4 feet apart. X1 throws to X2 who volleys on the laces back into X1's hands. X1 runs backwards three feet quickly and serves again. X2 meets ball and volleys again to X1. Repeat sequence.

Progression(s)

- Work half the length of the field
- Change places with partner and work back to the start
- Condition volleying foot - left then right
- Introduce controlling touch - Knee, chest, head - then volley etc

Key Factors

- Up on your toes - firm volleys with laces - toe pointed down - knee over ball
- Take quick steps forward and set up for next volley
- Vary height and weight of serves
- Keep serves coming quick
- Relax on controlling touch and set for volley

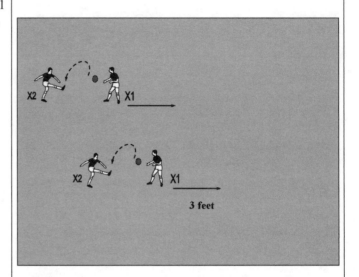

Organization - World Cup

All players stand in a circle. Any player starts the drill with a thigh volley of the ball into any other player. Players must keep the ball in the air without it hitting the ground.

Progression(s)

- Condition touches on players
  - head only
  - feet only
  - must have one touch
  - must have two touches
- Player who lets it drop is eliminated - play to a winner

Key Factors

- Be alert on your toes
- Relax and control the ball
- Try to make it harder for team mates
- Remember the rules - be ready for change

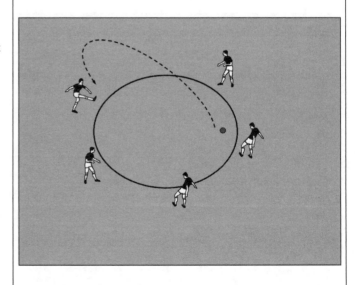

Dribbling

Feeling comfortable using all parts of the feet/keep your head up
- Sole of the feet
- Laces
- Inside of the foot
- Outside of the foot
- Manipulate the ball to do what you want it to do - Coerver skills
- Don't look down at the ball - know where it is by touch

Close Control
- Not too close to the body
- Ball always in stride length
- Shield ball from opponents

Change of pace / Change of direction
- Slowing into defenders
- Explode away
- Use of body swerve
- Create space and attack it
- Be able to go in different directions
- Comfortable with both feet

The ability to feint and dummy
- Use of moves - Matthews, Maradona, scissors, shuffle, Ronaldo etc.
- Time and space to use move
- Distance between you and defender
- Use of body to emphasise fake/dummy

- Decision Making - when and where to dribble
- Having and end product - shoot or pass after the dribble
- Attacking mentality - take players on

Dribbling

Organization - Square Relays

Two players line up in the corner of each square. The first players in each corner dribble to back player at the opposite corner who takes the ball and continues the drill. All four front players in each square go at the same time. The drill continues until all players return to starting positions. First team back wins

Progression(s) Condition Dribbling Technique

- Sole of the feet forwards
- Sole of the feet backwards
- Sideways
- Inside of feet
- Outside of feet
- Combination - Inside, outside sole
- Different turns in middle twice before continuing

Key Factors

- Close touches - Control with different areas of the feet
- Head up - Peripheral vision
- Change of speed
- Change of direction
- Do not cheat to win - Quality

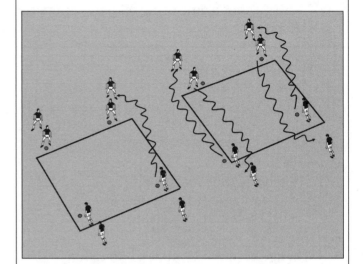

Organization - Fakes/Moves

Players in opposite corners dribble to middle - perform set move/fake and continue to opposite corner. Opposite corners do the same and repeat four times until players arrive back at original corners.

Progression(s)

- Matthews
- Maradona
- Shuffle
- Scissors
- Ronaldo

Key Factors

- Slowly in - Accelerate after move
- Close control - Use entire body for disguise
- Head up - quick feet
- Make sure both players go the same way

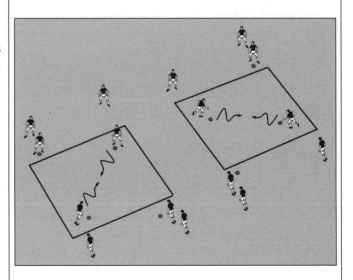

Dribbling

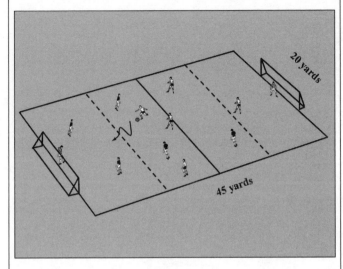

Organization

Two teams playing 6 v 6 must not pass backwards - they can advance forwards only by dribbling or running with the ball or taking a shot to score.

Progression(s)

- Divide fields into thirds - Players must stay in own zone unless they dribble into next zone
- Game can also be played 4 v 4

Key Factors

- Support from behind and decide early to dribble
- Be brave - take players on - accelerate into spaces on the field

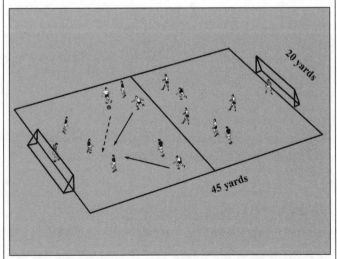

Organization

Set up as previous but now game is played 8 v 8 full scrimmage.

Progression(s)

- Highlight differences between dribbling and running with the ball - uses of each and when

Key Factors

- Can players dribble at the right times
- Reiterate four key factors of dribbling
- Dribble in the right areas of the field

Dribbling

Organization - Using the Body

Working in pairs, players face each other 2 ft apart without a ball. X1 has to try and get to either side marker before D1. Award points for each successful time.

Progression(s)

- Five times each and rotate positions
- Use hands then feet to touch the markers
- Introduce a ball - players must roll ball over marker before defenders can get a touch - keep score still

Key Factors

- Use the body - drop the shoulders, try to unbalance the defender
- Attack the half yard of space created, quickly
- Keep using the body when the ball is there - keep tight control
- Keep head up at all times

Organization - One on One

D1 passes to X1. X1 has to beat D1 and dribble to cone 1 or 2 at opposite end. D1 can close down after X1's first touch. Award points for successful dribbles and award points for tackle.

Progression(s)

- Make defender passive at first if attackers are struggling - then introduce active defending.
- Rotate players
- Change partners to increase competition
- Bring in a cone on side lines award point for dribbling there - two for getting to the end lines.

Key Factors

- Take good first touch out of your feet
- Be aware of space to attack and try to "get at" defender quickly
- Use fakes/moves to create space and always try to go forward with purpose
- Encourage creativity and positive attacking mentality

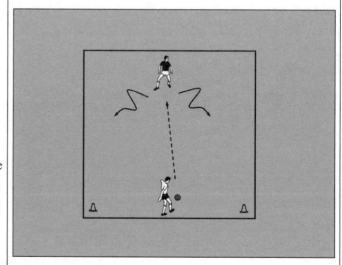

Dribbling

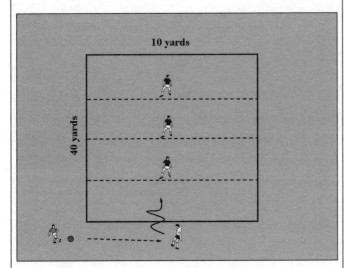

Organization - Run The Gauntlet
S1 plays ball to X1. X1 turns and dribbles at D1. X1 has to beat each defender to complete the gauntlet. D's can only move along the lines. If the ball goes out sideways - X restarts.

Progression(s)
- Use more defenders if you wish
- Rotate players in each positions
- Have S1 pressure X1 to first defender to increase sharpness of turn and ensure positive approach to drill.
- Adjust activeness of the defenders to get more success of attackers

Key Factors
- Attack defenders at speed
- Keep head up and use fakes/moves at correct angles and distance to/from defenders
- Try to vary moves - be creative, not predictable
- Try to create game like approach - pressure from S1 comes after first touch from the other side.

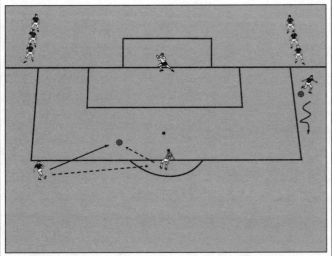

Organization - Dribble and Shoot
Two lines of players behind O1 and X1. X1 dribbles ball along edge of area - across front of area - plays one-two with coach and strikes at goal. O1 repeats from other side. Swap sides and continue. 1 point for each goal.

Progression(s)
- Make players perform set moves or tasks on each dribble
- Coach acts as a passive defender where players have to beat them to score
- Players have to roll coach with turn before shooting
- Condition shooting foot

Key Factors
- Keep head up and dribble at pace with purpose
- Use moves/fakes with confidence
- Concentrate on the strike after the skill
- Be aware of coaches position and then GK's and act accordingly.

Dribbling Games

Organization

Players dribble ball around square approximately 20 by 20 yards trying to avoid one another. On coaches number command, players perform relevant task.

Progression(s)

- #1 juggle with feet
- #2 juggle with knees
- #3 juggle with head
- After juggle ends players should continue to dribble

Key Factors

- Keep heads up and dribble into spaces
- Use different parts of the feet
- Relax on juggling - get balance and take soft, small touches

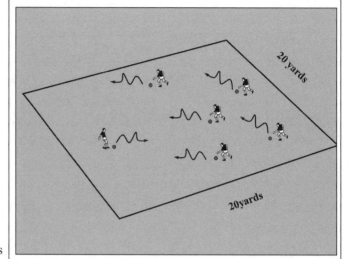

Organization

Set up as previous - players dribble around square trying to avoid one another. On coaches body part command, players to put that body part on the ball and hold it there.

Progression(s)

- Make last player to do task perform a certain skill - five juggles or ten toe taps on ball etc

Key Factors

- Players should keep close control at all times
- Try to perform task as soon as possible
- Try to catch everybody out
- Heads up - use all the area

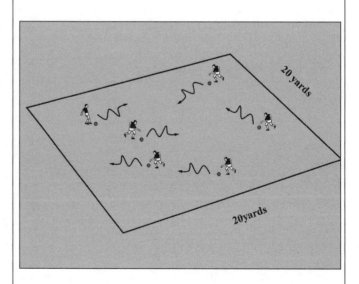

Dribbling Games

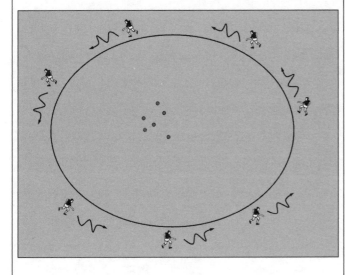

Organization
Players run around edge of circle approximately 15 yards in diameter (within the 20 by 20 yard square). On whistle, players run into middle of the circle, turn with the ball and dribble ball out of the circle. Players who get a ball stay in the game.

Progression(s)
• Players should try and challenge others if they do not get a ball
• Condition the turn for each round
• Allow losing players to judge the next round

Key Factors
• Players must perform a turn in the middle
• Players must dribble out of square
• Players must keep moving on outside
• Always have two winners

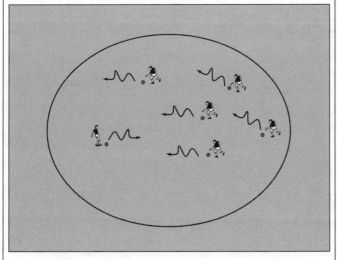

Organization - King of the Ring
Same set up as previous with players now dribbling inside of circle. On whistle players have to kick every other players ball out of the circle. If a players ball goes out of circle they are out of the game.

Progression(s)
• Players must not stand on edge of circle
• Players can not join up to get people out
• Players must not leave their balls unattended!!!

Key Factors
• Try to shield your ball whilst tackling for others
• Keep close control
• No rough tackling
• Always have two winners

Dribbling Games

Organization	Diagram

Organization
Players dribble in and around a 20 by 20 yard grid. On "go" command, X's dribble through as many gates as they can until coach shouts stop.

Progression(s)
- Limit time and try to beat last score
- X's have to stop ball between gate and change direction
- X's use gates as defenders and uses fake/moves to beat them

Key Factors
- Keep head up
- Use different parts of the feet
- Quick change of direction
- Decision making - If another player is already at a gate - find another open one quickly

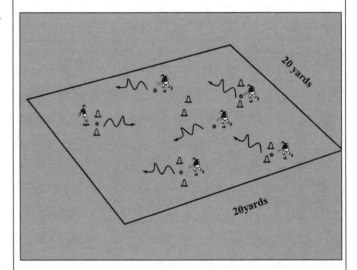

Organization
Same set up as above. Players now work in pairs and dribble and pass around the grid. On "go" command players have to see how many passes through gates they can make in a minute.

Progression(s)
- Award points for pass through each gate
- Minus a point if players hit markers on pass
- Limit time and try to beat previous score

Key Factors
- Keeps heads up
- Use different parts of the feet
- Quick changes of direction
- Decision making - If another player is already at a gate - find another open one quickly

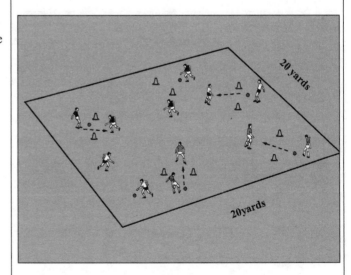

Dribbling Games

Organization

Each player has a ball and dribbles around listening for commands.

- Green light - fast
- Amber light - slow
- Red light - stop

If a players jumps red light - coach police chase and tap them

Progression(s)

- Players who get caught by police have to perform tasks
  - Ten toes taps
  - Ten juggles
  - Five headers
- Condition dribbling skill
- Bring in fakes/moves
- Let players be police

Key Factors

- Keep head up - find spaces
- Change pace and direction with commands
- Use skill to avoid police
- Keep close control so you don't have to foil police
- Use different parts of the feet to dribble

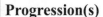

Organization

Players dribble ball within a 20 by 20 yard square. Two players come in and try to kick players balls out of the square. If a players ball goes out - they retrieve ball and come to middle of grid - open legs wide and place ball overhead until one of the other players dribble their ball through the players legs to release them.

Progression(s)

- Restrict time of play
- Condition dribbling skill
- Make players who are stuck perform a task before coming back into the square
  - Ten toes taps
  - Ten juggles
- Award points for players who are not stuck at the end

Key Factors

- Use different dribbling skills as you would in a game situation
- Fetch ball quickly if out and get friends to unstick you
- Avoid players kicking you out - shield the ball
- Only two players at a time kicking balls out of grid

Running With The Ball

Running with the ball is something many players will do in a game and is not to be confused with dribbling a ball - there are certain key differences between the two skills and when coaching players these differences need to be highlighted. Some of the key factors when running with the ball are:

- Players should use their peripheral vision - look ahead
- Strike the ball with the laces or instep
- Kick the ball a little distance in front and out of your stride
- Try to attack the space ahead of you as quickly as possible
- As with dribbling - Running with the ball is only a means to an end - remain composed to pass, cross, dribble or shoot

Decision Making

All of these factors come into deciding whether or not to run with the ball

- Have you got space in front of your opponent to run at them
- Is there space beyond your opponent to run into
- How quickly do you need to cover the distance
- How much space is available

To run as fast as they can with the ball players should use the instep or laces rather than the inside of the foot as this maintains your natural running stride pattern. Players should always be looking up and know their surroundings on the field but especially when running with the ball to avoid dangerous collisions.

Running With The Ball

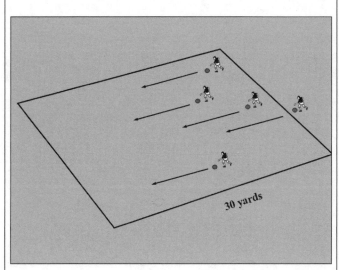

Organization
All players with a ball standing at one end of a 30 yard grid square. Players have to run with the ball to the opposite end of grid. Return to the same end on coaches command.

Progression(s)
- Condition to left foot only
- Right foot only
- Alternate
- Laces only
- Try to do in minimum of four - maximum of six touches in each direction
- Give time limits

Key Factors
- Good 1st touch out of feet
- Keep head up
- Use laces/instep
- Cover ground quickly and as straight as possible
- Keep ball out of feet but still under control

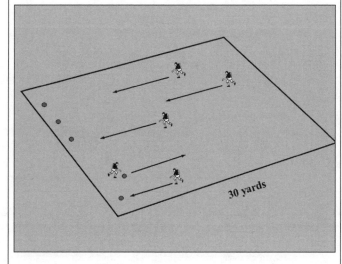

Organization
Same set up as above but with players lined up on opposite side to the balls. On "go" command, players run to opposite end - turn with ball and run back to start - stop the ball on the line. Coach kicks two balls out - repeat exercise.

Progression(s)
- Players have to compete to run with ball back
- Whoever stops ball on line stays in - if players don't get the ball first they must tackle
- Condition to left foot only, right foot only and alternate
- Limit number of touches allowed to complete a round

Key Factors
- React to "go" quickly
- Sprint to balls and be aware of opponents when turning
- Use good technique when running with the ball back
- Must stop ball on the line to show it is under control
- Fair play should be encouraged under competition

Running With The Ball

Organization

Two teams of equal numbers are split with half the numbers at each end of a 40 yard grid. A1 at top end begins running with the ball to A1 at bottom. A1 then runs up to A2 etc - keep going until back in starting position.

Progression(s)

- Race teams against each other
- Use more teams if involving large numbers
- Condition striking foot - left, right, alternate

Key Factors

- Good first touch out of feet
- Keep head up
- Use laces/instep
- Cover ground quickly and as straight as possible
- Must take a minimum of three touches - can only pass to next player from 10 ft or closer
- Must maintain control

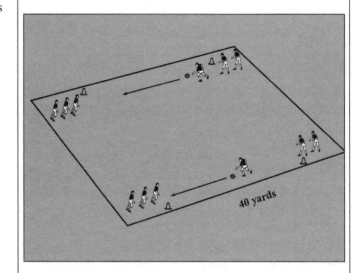

Organization

Four teams with players in number sequence as shown. Each number 1 has a ball and stands with number 5 in first corner of half field. Player 1 runs to player 2 - player 2 to 3 and so on - each round players will be in the next corner. Repeat until players are back in starting positions

Progression(s)

- First team back in starting positions wins
- Repeat with conditions for each leg i.e. 1st leg of race left foot only
- Teams should wear different color bibs

Key Factors

- Players should follow the technical aspects learned previously
- Do not run onto the field - no cutting corners
- Minimum of four touches between corners
- Do not kick any other teams ball
- Player 5 must stop ball in corner to show it is under control

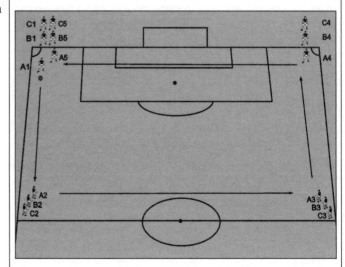

Running With The Ball

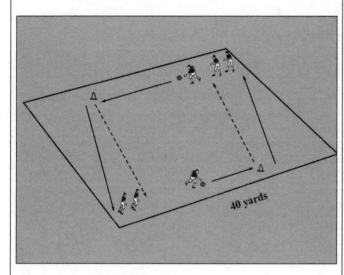

Organization

Players are split into two groups 40 yards apart. X runs with ball 30 yards then players pass square for O. O takes touch out of feet and runs before passing to X.

Progression(s)

- Condition to left foot only, right, alternate then laces only
- Try to do in minimum of four - maximum of six touches in each direction
- Limit time to complete

Key Factors

- Good first touch out of feet
- Keep head up
- Use laces/instep
- Cover ground quickly and as straight as possible
- Look up and make quality pass to next player

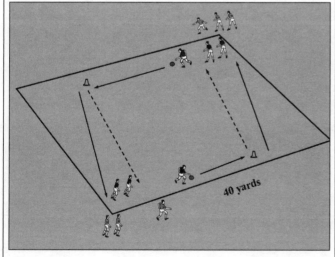

Organization

Same setup as previous but now with defenders. Once runner has taken first touch then defender tries to put pressure on that player and challenge for the ball. Award points for defenders if they clear ball out of grid.

Progression(s)

- Condition to left foot only, right, alternate then laces only
- Try to do in minimum of four - maximum of six touches in each direction
- Limit time to complete

Key Factors

- Even more important to take a good first touch out of feet
- Keep head up
- Use laces/instep
- Cover ground quickly and as straight as possible
- Look up and make quality pass to next player
- Don't panic with defender

Running With The Ball

Organization

Same principles as previous exercise with players split in groups working over 40 yard dimension - now with end product. X runs with ball down line then delivers cross for O who makes supporting run. O finishes cross into goal - players stay at this end - next X and O go in opposite direction

Progression(s)

- Players should alternate from crosser to finisher
- Use left and right sides for running and crossing
- Introduce defenders for each players as in previous exercise
- Increase supporting runners to two
- Add in a goalkeeper

Key Factors

- Player should continue using the techniques learned from previous exercise and now concentrate on delivering a good cross after their hard work
- Work on running with the ball style rather than finishing or support runs but success breeds confidence, so aid if needed
- Players should be looking at support runners position as they attack flanks
- Look up before crossing

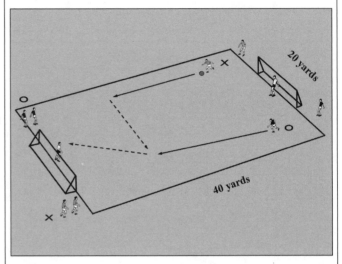

Organization

A normal scrimmage is set up with play being 4 v 4, 6 v 6 or 8 v 8. Wide zones are added where players can not be challenged.

Progression(s)

- Introduce thirds of the field if necessary and make players advance only by running with the ball
- Take away zones and neutral wide areas

Key Factors

- Players should make use of the wide zones to run into space and hurt opponents
- When games are introduced, players should be reminded of the need to still be technically sound

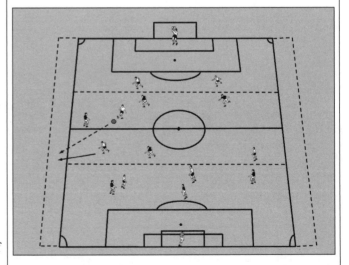

Running With The Ball

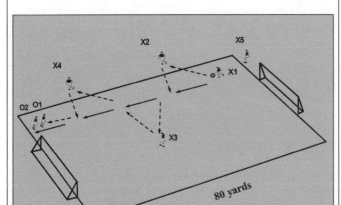

Organization

X1 runs along touch line and plays one-two with X2. X1 takes pass out into stride and continues to play one-twos with X3 and X4 before passing to O1. O1 repeats the sequence in the opposite direction. Use both wings if larger group.

Progression(s)

- Change the middle servers
- Condition use of each foot and limit touches
- Take the third one-two inside so player then heads towards goal and must finish
- Introduce a goalkeeper then defender so players are under pressure when shooting after long run with the ball

Key Factors

- Keep heads up and cover space quickly
- Make good crisp passes and take receiving touch out into stride
- Finish with good weight of pass into the next runner to allow drill to run smoothly
- When shooting is brought in - relax and concentrate on quality of finish
- Do not panic with pressure

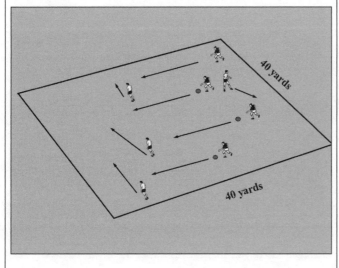

Organization

Play takes place in a 40 by 40 yard grid with players split into two groups X's and O's. X's have to run with ball across grid square while O's walk around without a ball - X's have to avoid collisions and find space.

Progression(s)

- Rotate players
- Allow O's to jog then sprint
- Limit controlling feet
  - left foot only
  - right foot only
  - alternate feet

Key Factors

- Head up - look for spaces
- Attack space in front with speed
- Use least amount of touches possible
- Use laces/outside of feet
- Attack space side to side of defenders and between them

Running With The Ball

Organization

In a 40 by 40 yard grid, two teams of six players play keep away with players encouraged to run with the ball. Players must be three yards or less from a defender before passing.

Progression(s)

- Bring in end zones to score - players score by finding another player with a pass in other teams end zone
- Bring in goals and play first team to five goals
- Keep passing rule of less than three yards

Key Factors

- Players are encouraged to run at defenders - be aware of space ahead and between defenders
- Attacking mentality - get at defenders before passing and moving
- Always be looking at your position - space around you

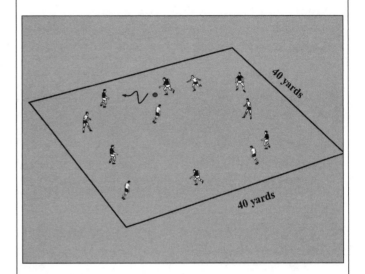

Organization

A 30 by 45 yard field is split into thirds with players lined up as shown in diagram. The goalkeeper throws a ball to X1/X2/X3 and they combine to free one player up who runs with the ball into the next zone or attacking third. Player can use X4 or not and X's try to score past O's - O's attack opposite end.

Progression(s)

- Only player with the ball can advance into next zone
- Encourage players to spread out and rotate each outfield positions
- Allow one support runner to assist player running with the ball
- Take out zones

Key Factors

- Positive first touch
- Decision making - if space attack it quickly - if not - pass to player in space and support
- Good technique - laces
- Movement off the ball - i.e. can X4 peel away to allow space for runner to attack
- Take shooting chances

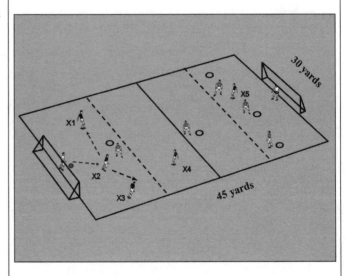

Shooting/Attacking Play

Technique
- Non-kicking foot beside the ball
- Strike ball on laces
- Knee over the ball
- Shoulder over the ball
- Head over the ball
- Keep your head steady
- Point your toe where you want the ball to go

Considerations
- Striking a moving ball
- Approaching the ball from an angle
- Aiming across the goal to the far post
- Correct body shape to strike
- Sweeping the ball into the goal
- Accuracy before power
- Strike at earliest opportunity

Other Related Topics
- Finishing
- Decision making - type of finish - side foot, lob, power strike, beat the keeper
- One on one's

Attacking Play
- Combinations
- Attacking runs - key areas
- Working in pairs - roles of each attacker
- Movement off the ball
- Creating space
- Greediness - hunger to score a goal
- Using your body - pinning defenders
- Taking players on

Shooting

Organization

X1 stands - X2 kneels only 3 feet away. X2 rolls ball to X1 who strikes ball back to X2. X2 stops and rolls quickly to X1's opposite foot. Try to work partner fast and hard.

Progression(s)

- X1 and X2 reverse rolls
- Limit time and count number of touches
- Compare scores on each foot - try to better each time
- Increase distance between players to 5 ft

Key Factors

- Up on your toes and quick steps between strikes
- Knee over ball - toes pointed down
- Strike on the laces - follow through to target
- Accuracy before power

Organization

X1 shoots at X2's goal. X2 tries to save and then shoots back at X1. Goals only count if below knee height. Goalkeepers may not use hands.

Progression(s)

- Players roll ball to the side and try to strike to opposite corner of goal
- Limit to two touches
- Alternate feet
- X1's roll ball for X2's to hit back at them - swap

Key Factors

- Knee, shoulder, head over the ball. Non kicking foot beside the ball
- Approach from an angle
- Shoot low and to the corners
- Look at goalkeepers positioning before you shoot

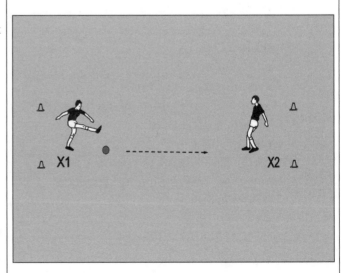

Shooting

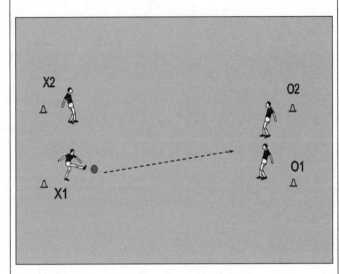

Organization
X1 rolls ball to the side an shoots at opposite end goal. O1 and O2 try to save not using hands and then shoot back at X's goal. First team to five goals wins.

Progression(s)
- Limit to two touches per player
- Partners must play one-two before shooting
- Limit to three touches per team with the set-up
- Allow goalkeepers to use hands and increase distance

Key Factors
- Quality of technique - test the goalkeepers
- Work on angles for the lay off in the one-two's
- Work as a team, catch opponents off guard with quick returns
- Keep accuracy as power increases with distance

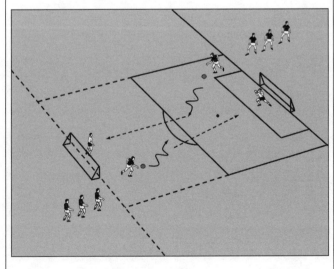

Organization
X1 and O1 dribble ball to center of square. Players use move and take ball to the right. Players shoot and try to beat goalkeepers. Players join end of opposing teams line.

Progression(s)
- Players have to use different fake/move each time
- Make players take ball to left as well as right
- Bring in passive then active defenders
- Play ball in from opposite corner then players attack the goals

Key Factors
- Concentrate on the shot after the move
- Keep head up and decide early what you will do
- Attack with pace and purpose
- Work on both feet and taking the ball both ways past the defenders

Shooting

Organization - Hitting the Corners

X1 and X2 each have a goal with markers indicating bottom corners. Players take alternate shots trying to score. Keep score - 1 point for each goal, 3 points in corners

Progression(s)
- Shoot standing still
- Hit a moving ball
- Partners play you the ball - then control and shoot
- Condition shooting foot
- Increase distance apart

Key Factors
- Approach at an angle
- Keep knee, head and shoulder over the ball
- Strike with laces across the goal
- Use both feet
- Look at keepers position

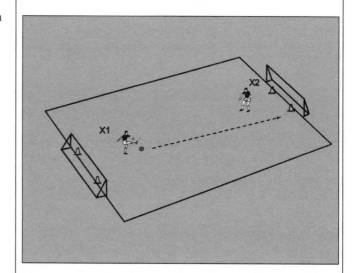

Organization - One on One

Work in pairs twenty feet apart. X1 passes to X2 from 5 feet behind the goal. When X2 takes first touch, X1 goes into the goal. X2 tries to score past X1 - who must not use hands at first. Point for each goal

Progression(s)
- Limit shooting player to two touches
- Limit shooting player to one touch
- Vary height and weight of passes
- allow X1 to use hands
- Condition striking foot
- Condition controlling touch

Key Factors
- X1 must not defend/keep until X2 touches ball
- Take first touch out of feet
- Approach strike at an angle
- Look at keepers position
- Use fakes/moves to unbalance X1
- Strike through on the laces
- Keep ball low

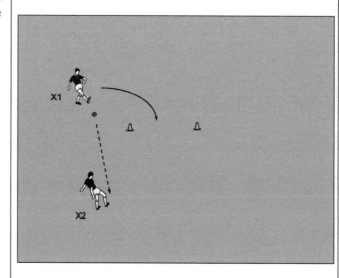

Shooting

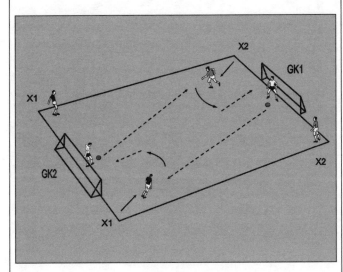

Organization - Turn and Shoot

Two teams of three play with 1 goalkeeper and two forwards in opposite corners. GK1 rolls ball to either x1 at opposite end 20 feet away. X1 has to meet pass, turn and shoot at GK2. GK2 then rolls ball into either X2 to beat GK1. Repeat.

Progression(s)

- Vary height and pace of delivery from GK's
- Make players strike moving ball
- Let both X1's team up to beat GK2 and both X2's take on GK1
- Limit players touches
- Condition controlling touch and set ups

Key Factors

- Meet the ball quickly and get quick shot on the turn
- Importance of first touch
- Angled approach after touch - set to shoot
- Look at keepers positioning as you set for strike
- Keep strike low - early decisions on type of strike

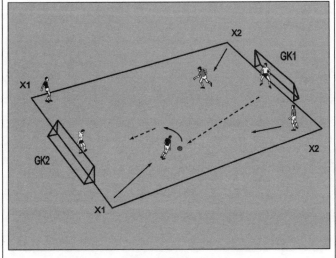

Organization - Turn and Shoot Under Pressure

Same set up as previous but as X1 meets pass from GK1 - X2's can challenge attackers after 1st touch.

Progression(s)

- Vary height and pace of delivery from GK's
- Passive then active defending
- Let both X1's team up to beat GK2 and both X2's take on GK1
- Let both defend against opponents

Key Factors

- Meet the ball quickly and get quick shot on the turn
- Try to get body between you and defenders coming at you
- Defenders try and get goal side quickly
- Combine with partner - use quick and varied combination play

Shooting

Organization

Four lines of players with equal numbers line up as shown. X1's pass ball to O1's who shoot first time at the goal. Players swap lines. X2's then serve to O2's who shoot and the drill continues in sequence.

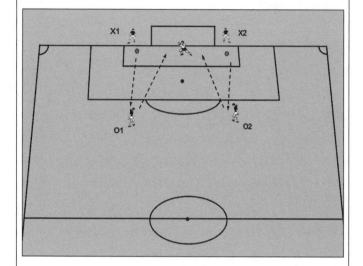

Progression(s)

• Make players swap sides
• Players throw balls for volleys
• Players chip balls in for partners to control and shoot
• Bring in a goalkeeper and/or passive defenders

Key Factors

• Quality of service into strikers
• Angle of approach to the ball
• Aim for opposite corners
• Follow through and react for rebounds
• Look at GK's positioning

Organization

Set up as previous but with X1 and O1 and X2 and O2 diagonally opposite. X1's pass ball to O1's who shoot first time at the goal. Players swap lines. X2's then serve to O2 who shoots and drill continues in sequence.

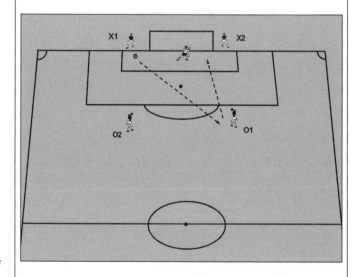

Progression(s)

• Players swap sides
• Players throw balls in for volleys then chip ball in to control and shoot
• Vary service position - put them wider for full on crosses
• Bring in a goalkeeper and/or defenders

Key Factors

• Serves or crosses must be at good pace to hit
• Make an early decision on the strike depending on service
• Control out of feet to set up strike
• Shoot low and across the goalkeeper

Shooting

Organization

Servers line up around outside of goal area with an even number on each side at each station. Server X1 on the left passes to S2 who shoots first time. Server X1 on the right passes to S1 who shoots first time. Continue serves to same strikers with servers X2 through X4.

Progression(s)

- Every player to play in each position
- Condition strikers to shoot with nearest foot and weaker foot
- Condition striker to use furthest foot and allow ball to come across the body
- Make servers throw-in balls
- Add a goalkeeper

Key Factors

- Strike with laces - watch ball onto foot
- Curve approach to the ball
- Angle yourself to goal - sweep ball into net
- Quick feet - adjust to flight of service
- Aim across the goal
- Look at goalkeepers positioning

Organization

Two goals are positioned forty yards apart. S1 dribbles forward - passes square for D who supports and shoots first time - swap ends and positions. S2 then serves for A. S3 serves for C. S4 serves for B and repeat.

Progression(s)

- Players change from servers to strikers
- Widen or lengthen grid to stretch players more
- Bring in goalkeepers
- Time/touch conditions on goals

Key Factors

- Keep drill at fast pace
- Time and angle of strikers runs
- Good body shape to shoot
- Quality and varied services
- Key areas to shoot at
- Communication between servers and shooters

Shooting

Organization
Two lines of equal players X's and O's. X dribbles ball to cone from flank position. Players play ball inside of cone - run around the outside of cone and shoot at goal past GK.

Progression(s)
• Players should take turns on alternate sides
• Put time limit on players
• Limit to two touches after the dribble - one to pass - one to shoot
• Add a defender who becomes active after pass around cone

Key Factors
• Attack drill at pace
• Pass should set up a first time shot
• Plan your shot as you run around cone - look up and see where GK's position is
• Follow ball in for rebounds
• Shot must be accurate - hit the target

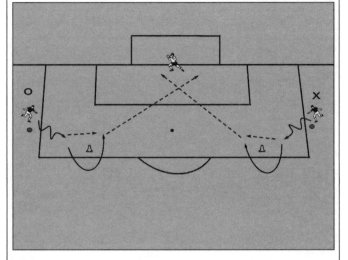

Organization
X1 passes to X2. X2 plays one-two with X3 and turns into space ahead to shoot the return pass. Players rotate to the next position.

Progression(s)
• Move X2 to the other side of the area and create new passing and shooting angles
• Limit players to two touch - then one touch
• Bring in a defender to pressure X2's pass but allow to spin and shoot

Key Factors
• Encourage quick one touch play
• Quality of passing - weight and accuracy
• Quick spin by X2 and hit shot first time
• Be inventive if things go wrong - play as you see it - especially with defenders

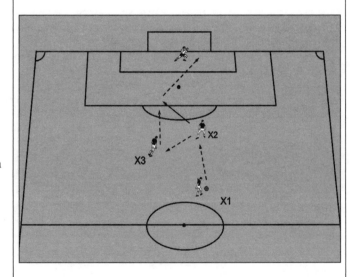

Shooting

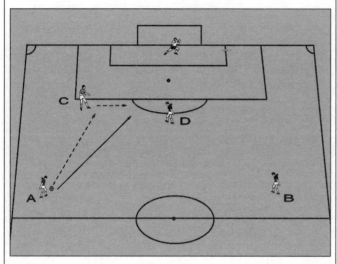

Organization - Long Wall Pass and Shoot

Two lines of players at A and B. One attacker C at edge of penalty area. A begins by driving ball into C - following for return pass and shooting at goal to beat GK. B repeats from opposite side.

Progression(s)

- Players should rotate sides after each turn
- Introduce attacker D who receives first pass from C and lays ball ahead for onrushing A or B to shoot first time
- Limit to one touch all round except for C who may take controlling touch
- Add a defender if ability allows

Key Factors

- First pass sets up the drill so must be quality - drive ball in to C
- Run hard to get on the end of return pass and strike at goal first time
- Look at GK's position as you run - plan strike and execute
- Lay off should be one touch from D and well weighted

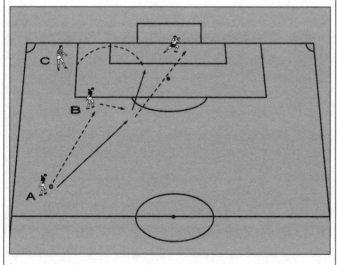

Organization

Similar set up as previous but a little closer to goal. A plays one-two with B and shoots past GK. A then runs in for a header with delivery from player C. Next player becomes player A and all players rotate to next position.

Progression(s)

- Have deliveries coming in from different angles and from both sides of the area
- Limit to one touch
- Award points for each goal scored and for each save

Key Factors

- Quick interchange of passes and early strike
- Look at GK's position as you run in
- Attack for header at pace - try to aim down - need for good flighted delivery
- Change roles quickly and keep drill moving at pace

Shooting

Organization
Teams of four play on a 30 by 20 yard field with a supply of balls in each goal. GK throws ball in to the team - they have three touches to score past their opponents - they must stay in their own half - game continues

Progression(s)
- First team to five goals wins
- limit teams to one touch finishes
- Stipulate every player must touch the ball in the three touches
- Add an extra player to each team who is only allowed in opponents half

Key Factors
- Get shots off quickly
- Try to set up play for the one touch finish
- Communication between teams
- Keepers should restart quickly
- Aim away from the GK's - low and in the corners - catch the other team out

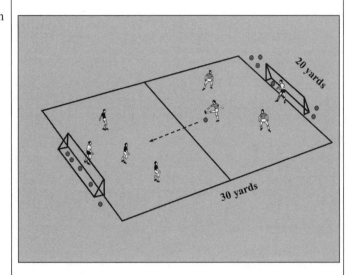

Organization
Line up with one striker (X), one GK and eight servers (as shown in the diagram). X runs in receives a pass going away from them from A1 - X shoots first time - runs back around marker and repeats with pass from A2. B1 and B2 play square pass for X to hit. C1 and C2 play passes coming at X and D1 and D2 serve ball in the air for X to volley.

Progression(s)
- X must run around marker in between each shot
- X must striker left foot from all passes from 1's and right footed from 2's
- Keep count of goals scored and time taken to complete test

Key Factors
- Quick running between strikes
- Concentrate on making good contact for each strike with either foot
- Remain composed throughout
- While running look at GK's position
- React to each pass quickly

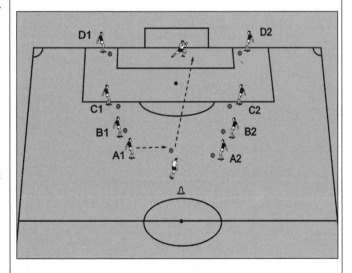

Shooting

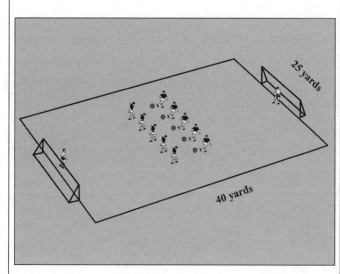

Organization

Players work in pairs 5 feet apart with goals 40 yards apart. Players perform task set by coach - when number is shouted player with the ball has to turn and shoot past GK's. Continue until all players have shot at goal a few times.

Progression(s)

- One touch passing
- One touch juggling
- Headers
- Rotate partners after each round and rotate GK's ends

Key Factors

- Work hard on the skill tasks and be alert for when number is called
- React quickly to number and turn to shoot
- look at GK's position - compose yourself and pick your spot
- Retrieve ball quickly and continue with skills

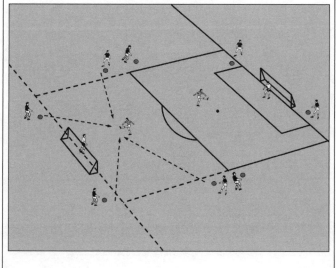

Organization

Two goals with GK's and eight server (S) each with a supply of balls. 2 Strikers X and O. Servers play ball in on coaches command at varied height and paces. X and O have to finish past GK's.

Progression(s)

- Limit finishes to two or one touch depending on ability
- Have serves thrown or kicked in depending on ability
- Bring in a second striker and allow rebounds - encourage following in

Key Factors

- Game like serves and reactions
- Strikers should be alert and adjust to each delivery quickly
- Select type of finish early - header - toe poke - volley and execute
- Be aware of GK's position

Shooting

Organization - Wide Angled Shooting

Three lines of players and a GK. X1 rolls ball forward and strikes at goal. X2 and X3 follow in for rebounds. Players rotate to next line as drill continues.

Progression(s)

- Reverse drill to opposite side of area
- Add a defender who starts beside X1 and reacts after X1's first touch
- Add second and third defender who mark up X2 and X3

Key Factors

- Take first touch out of feet - this will eliminate defender
- Keep your head up - look at GK's position
- Strike across the goal - low and hard to the far post
- Quick follow in runs - come in at an angle - curved runs draw defenders away
- Defenders pass ball back to GK to score

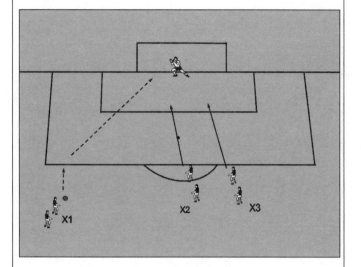

Organization

Two lines of players and a GK. S plays a pass ahead of X to take on and shoot past GK. S tries to make recovery run and thwart X's goal attempt. Rotate positions.

Progression(s)

- Vary height and weight of deliveries from S
- Limit number of touches X can have
- Add an extra defender who chases from just behind X

Key Factors

- Positive first touch out of feet towards goal
- Look at GK's position
- Early decision - pass into goal, chip GK, drive across goal - dribble around GK
- Follow in for rebounds
- Be aware of recovering defenders

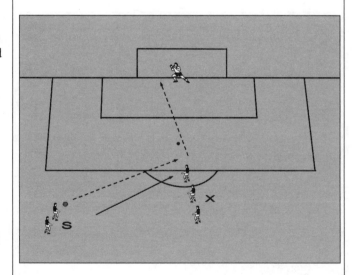

Shooting Games

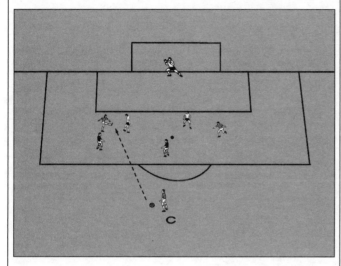

Organization - Wembley
Teams of two and a GK wait inside the goal area. Coach (C) serves ball into area and teams try to score to advance to next round. Goals cannot be scored inside the six yard area.

Progression(s)
- Lose one or two teams each round until you are left with two teams for a final
- Teams must score two goals in the final to win
- Limit to one touch finishes and two touch play
- Both players have to score in the final to win

Key Factors
- Work hard to get the ball and work with team mate
- Take shooting opportunities early
- Do not try to beat everybody - pass and move
- Be aware of opponents and GK's positioning

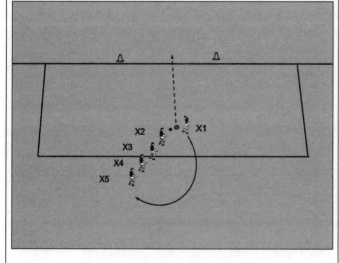

Organization - The Wall Game
Place two large stand up markers against a wall. X1 begins the game by shooting between cones and hitting the wall. X2 must hit the moving ball in one touch back between the markers and then its X3's turn etc.

Progression(s)
- Players join end of line after each shot
- Players are out of game if
  - They shoot outside the cones
  - If they take more than one touch
  - If the ball stops moving
- Play until you have a winner

Key Factors
- Try to shoot at an angle and with power - making it more difficult for the next player
- Get in line with the ball early and look up before shooting
- Adjust to last players shot quickly - give yourself time to strike it properly

Shooting Games

Organization - Wild West Shoot-out

Players are divided into two equal teams both facing a goalkeeper. Players are lined up side by side parallel to the penalty spot. Players take three steps back and on "go" - in sequence run and shoot - relay format.

Progression(s)
• Most goals per team wins - bonus goal for fastest team
• Must touch next players hand before they run up and shoot
• Make players use weaker foot
• Make players lay, sit, kneel, push up etc before shooting

Key Factors
• It's a race - do not collect ball or admire your shot
• Hit the target
• Make sure you touch your next shooter
• Be aware of opposition and goalkeeper
• Celebrate winning each round with wild gusto!!!

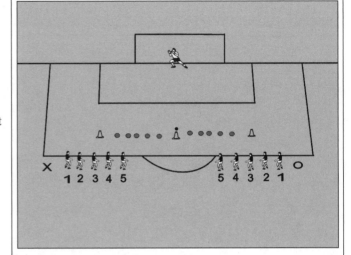

Organization - Shooter, Keeper, Shagger

Two equal teams line up just outside penalty area with a server nominated for each team. SX passes ball square for X1 to shoot first time at GKO. SO then passes to O1 who shoots at X1 who has become the goalkeeper.

Progression(s)
• Players continue in sequence - first shooting, then saving - then retrieving their ball back to their teams server
• Servers must always have a supply of balls and keep passes going quickly
• First team to ten wins

Key Factors
• React quickly - shoot then save - then fetch
• Quality serves = quality shots - keep passes quick
• Be aware of other team - get in position quickly
• Accuracy before power
• Shoot before goalie is ready - in corners

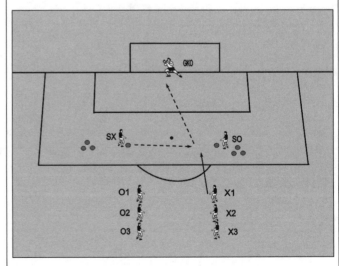

Shooting Games

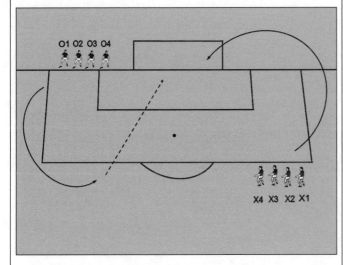

Organization
Two lines of players one behind the goal and the other at the edge of the area as shown. When numbers get called, players run around the edge of area to opposite side. O's take shots and X's have to save them. Players then swap sides so both can shoot and save.

Progression(s)
- One number at a time - left foot - then right
- Increase numbers competing and add in more balls
- Throw balls into strikers after they run so they must control and shoot
- Bring in time and touch restrictions

Key Factors
- Quick reactions when your number is called
- It's a race - run hard
- Compose yourself before shooting - look at where opponent is
- Aim away from the goalkeeper - low/corners
- Follow in for rebounds

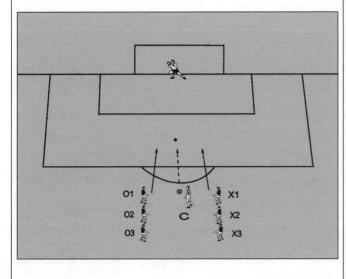

Organization
Two lines of players with coach standing between them line up outside of goal area. Coach serves ball ahead of players who race to shoot past the goalkeeper. Play until a goal is scored or ball goes out of play.

Progression(s)
- Serve balls in from different serving positions
  - Ahead of players
  - From the side
  - Chipped from behind
- Players lay on backs
- Push up position
- Laying on front
- Time/touches limited

Key Factors
- Quick reactions
- Use body to beat opponent
- Once ahead relax and concentrate on the shot
- Play until finish - tackle and keep shooting
- Technique must be good when tired and under pressure

Attacking

Organization - 1 v 1 Attacking

Within a 10 by 10 yard grid, X1 passes to X2. X2 controls and tries to dribble past X1's end line. X1 can close down and tackle only after X2's first touch. Award a point for every time they beat the defender.

Progression(s)
- Increase grid length to 20 yards and award points for halfway mark and double for attacking the end line
- Award points for tackle
- Rotate players after five attempts
- Change partners

Key Factors
- Take good first touch out of feet and attack defender at pace
- Keep control of the ball whilst maintaining good speed
- Use fakes/moves to create half yard of space and explode into it
- Be aware of defenders positioning

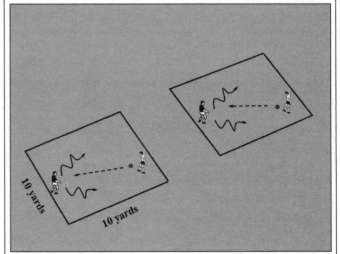

Organization - 2 v 2 Attacking

Similar set up as previous but now in a 20 by 20 yard grid. X1's pass to either of the X2's. X2's work together to try and dribble past X1's end line. X1's can only move to defend after X2's first touch. Points are awarded for every time they beat defenders.

Progression(s)
- Award points for defenders clearing
- Rotate pairs and partners to test players
- Bring in goal for attackers to shoot at
- Bring in a goalkeeper

Key Factors
- As above but work as a team - movement off the ball
- Communication and creativity - look for give and go's and overlaps etc.
- Remain poised to finish after beating defenders
- Good choice of finish

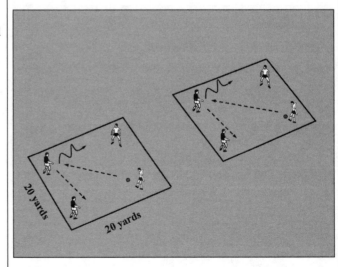

Diagram	Organization

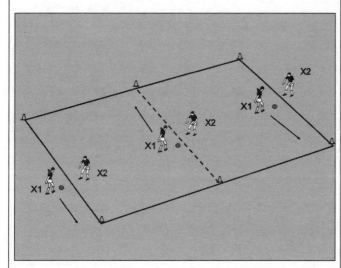

Organization - 1 on 1 Fake and Bake

X1 and X2 face each other 2 feet apart. Two markers at the side of them five feet away each side. Players have to dribble to either marker and stop ball to score a point. Most points after two minutes moves up a grid - loser moves down a grid.

Progression(s)

- If players draw - player who scored first moves up a grid
- After a goal is scored - ball goes to partner to continue
- As soon as ball is moved players can tackle
- Players may return to the same goal twice in a row as can opponent

Key Factors

- Use fakes/moves/dummies - to unbalance your opponent
- You only need half a yard to attack - explode into the space
- Keep close control to stop ball at marker
- Catch defender out and return to the same marker
- Use the body to do fakes and unbalance defender

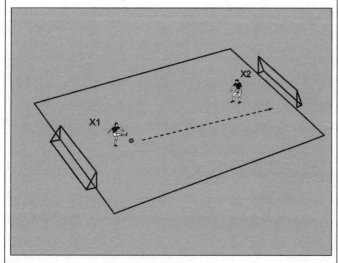

Organization

1 v 1 on a 20 by 10 yard game field. Players compete against each other for two minutes. After two minutes partners play.

Progression(s)

- Rotate players and partners on each field
- Increase to 2 v 2 then 3 v 3 and finally 4 v 4
- Introduce goalkeepers at any stage

Key Factors

- Have a positive attacking mind set
- Take players on
- Explode into space
- Use fakes and moves
- Never be afraid to shoot

Crossing

Organization - Striking The Ball
In groups of three, players pass the ball in a short, short long sequence.

Progression(s)
- Work on driven pass
- Curled pass around middle player

Key Factors
- Move into position early to allow for next pass
- Control and weight of pass must be very good
- Communication between players

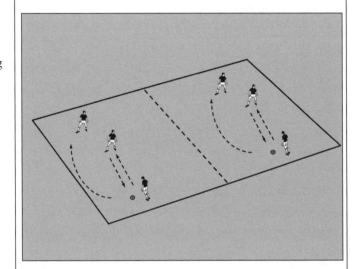

Organization - Three line Crossing
Players line up in lines just inside one half of a field as shown. 3a plays ball down line for 4a to deliver cross on the overlap. 1a and 2a make overlapping run into area to finish. All rotate one line to the right.

Progression(s)
- Progress to crossing from both sides
- Add a fifth line and have a deep midfield runner - crosser fakes first cross, takes to byline and pulls ball back for the late runner

Key Factors
- Call for ball on the overlap
- Angled approach to ball - do not get square to end line
- Pick player out before delivery
- Head down and concentrate on correct strike of the ball into key areas
- Quality of timing and runs to meet crosses
- Key areas to deliver into

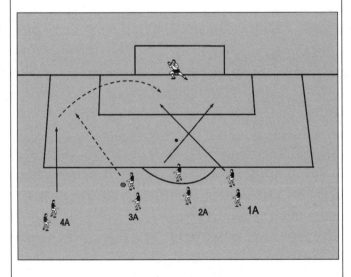

Crossing

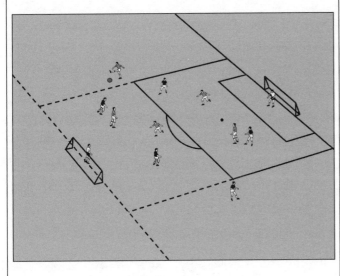

Organization - 4 v 4

Game is played with unopposed wide zones. GK A rolls ball into wide zone for early delivery from A1 to two remaining team mates. As soon as move breaks down, defending team then attacks opposite goal beginning with the GK B.

Progression(s)

• Allow play to continue without having to start from GK's

Key Factors

• Pick player out before delivery
• Quick transition from defense into attack - get ball in early before defenders settle
• Key areas to deliver into

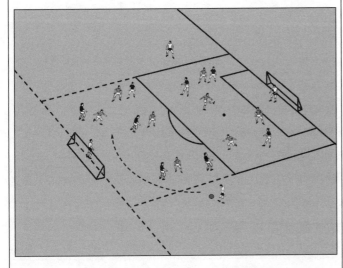

Organization

8 v 8 full scrimmage with unopposed wide zones. Players in wide zones play for both teams and cannot be challenged. Goals must be scored from a cross to count.

Progression(s)

• Players must make overlapping runs in order to cross from the wide zone
• Defenders allowed in wide zone

Key Factors

• Quality of delivery
• Ball between defender and goalkeeper
• Quality of runs
• Timing of runs
• Work the overlap
• Switch the field early using neutral players

Crossing And Finishing

Organization

Three player drill starting from the edge of the penalty area. X passes ball to S and make overlapping run around O. S passes back to O and O plays ball wide for X to run onto and then makes cross over run with S to finish cross.

Progression(s)

- All players rotate each position
- Use both flanks
- Limit players time or touches
- Bring in passive then active defenders

Key Factors

- Accuracy and weight of passing
- Timing of wide pass
- Timing of overlap and runs into the area
- Attack the key areas and provide a finish
- Composure after runs to execute cross/finish

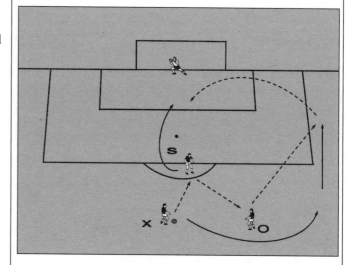

Organization

Three lines of players positioned just outside penalty area. C1 plays ball ahead of them down the line - runs onto the ball and delivers an outswinging cross. X1 and O1 make cross over run and try to finish cross past the goalkeeper.

Progression(s)

- Players after each turn rotate to the next line on the right
- Use both flanks
- Make crossers (C) fake move and deliver inswinging crosses
- Condition finishes to head, volley, control and finish etc
- Bring in defenders

Key Factors

- Good delivery on the run
- Swing ball away from goalkeeper into forwards path
- Angle and timing of runs into the area
- Body shape and adjustment to make the finish
- Quick decisions for quality of striker - power or finesse

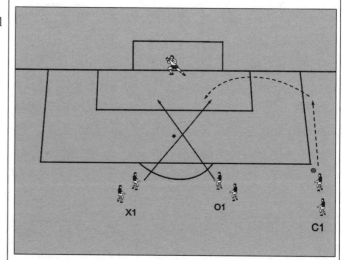

Crossing And Finishing

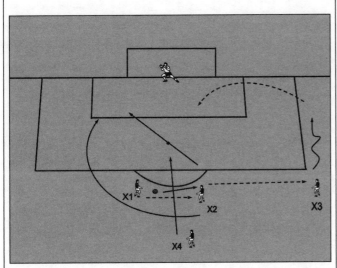

Organization

Four lines of players with equal numbers. X1 plays to X2 who stops ball and spins away. X1 follows on to pass to X3 and spins away. X3 runs onto pass from X1 and delivers cross for X1, X2 and X4 to attack. All players move to the right on completion.

Progression(s)

- Use left and right flanks for crossing
- Bring in overlap from extra player with X3
- Make X3 fake and take to by-line before pulling back for late run of X4
- Bring in central defenders - active
- Bring in passive wide defenders

Key Factors

- Quick interchange and movement between X1 and X2
- Good weight and direction of pass ahead of X3
- Communication between players
- Good deliveries to target players
- Accelerate to finish
- Play till a finish - rebounds

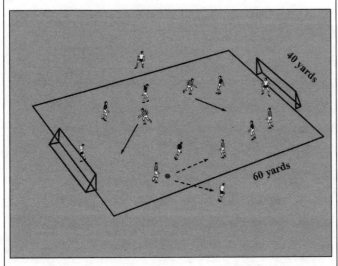

Organization

Two teams of six (including goalkeepers) play within a 60 by 40 yard game field with two wide zones. Two neutral players play in the wide zone area and play for the team in possession. The object is to score against opponents from a cross by either neutral player.

Progression(s)

- Limit game to two touch play
- Install one touch finish rule
- Rotate wide players every five minutes
- Allow defenders into wide zones

Key Factors

- Get ball wide early
- Play ball into space for wide players
- No straight runs for finishes
- Switch from defense into attack quickly

Finishing

Organization - Body Shape for Finishing

Players line up in threes, five feet between each player. X1 begins with ball in hand and serves to X2 who completes task into X3's hands. X3 then serves and continues. Rotate middle player after one minute for each task. X2 is sideways on and always plays across his body.

Progression(s)

- Players have to perform the following tasks
  - Outside of the thigh - volley
  - Inside of the thigh - volley
  - Outside of the foot - volley
  - Inside of the foot - volley

Key Factors

- Rotation of knee and groin above the hip - then rotation of the hip
- Up on toes ready for the volley
- Good strike of the ball into partners hand - set ready for next volley

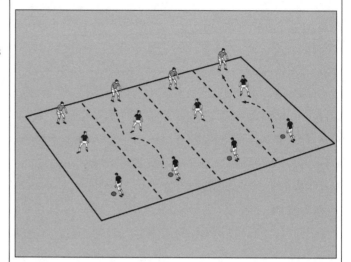

Organization - Directional Volleying

X1 serves to X2 to volley to X3. X3 then serves to X1 to volley to X2. X2 catches and serves to X3 to volley to X1.

Progression(s)

- Right foot only
- Left foot only

Key Factors

- Correct body positioning - 45 degree angle
- See where ball is coming from and where it is going to
- Rotation of the knee hip then laces volley
- Non kicking foot pointed to target area
- Sweep ball across body
- Correct approach to the ball - do not get square to the goal

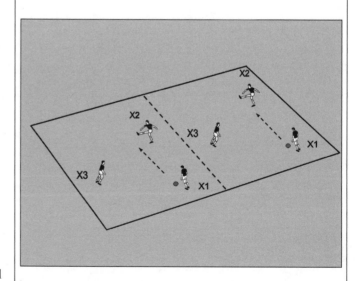

Finishing

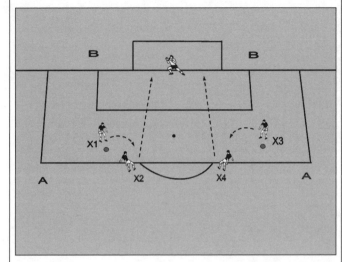

Organization - Functional Practice

X1 serves ball up for X2 to strike on goal and swap positions. X3 then serves ball up for X4 to finish and swap positions. Make sure players have turns at both left and right side of goal

Progression(s)

- Start with underarm throw and then vary height and weight of the delivery - all from area A
- Move onto chipped delivery from service area B

Key Factors

- Non kicking foot pointed to target area
- Repetition of technique from earlier drills
- Aim across the goals to far post
- Judge weight of pass and determine type of finish
- Body shape and follow through

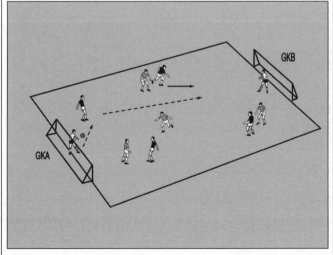

Organization

Ball starts with GK A who rolls ball into A team who have three touches per team to finish - must be first time strike at goal which scores. GK B attempts to save and immediately distributes to his team and continues.

Progression(s)

- Progress into 8 v 8 and maintain one touch finish rule to score

Key Factors

- Always look to finish at earliest opportunity
- Angle of support for pass and set up
- Head up early to see goalkeeper
- Decide on type of finish early and execute

Defending

- Deny time and space for opponents
- Pressure first touch
- Close down space quickly
- Jockey opponents
- Force player wide
- tackle opponent correctly
- Start the attack

Topics to cover
- Role of first defender
- Role of covering defender
- Role of balancing defender
- Defending as a unit
- Defending from the front
- Tackling
- The slide tackle
- Defensive heading
- Playing in a back four
- Playing in a back three

Decision Making
- When to mark - when to drop off
- Showing a player inside - outside
- When to commit a challenge
- Playing the offside trap

Defending

Diagram	Organization

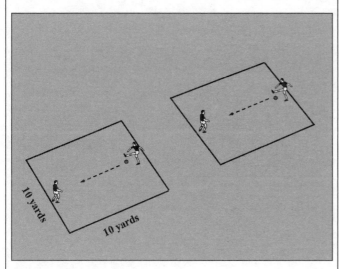

Organization - 1 v 1 Defending

In a 10 by 10 yard grid, X1 passes to X2. X2 controls and tries to dribble past X1's end line. X1 can close down and tackle after X2's first touch only. Award a point for every tackle.

Progression(s)

- Increase grid length to 20 yards and encourage patience and jockeying before the tackle
- Award points for attackers
- Rotate players after five
- Change partners

Key Factors

- Close down space quickly - slow down and get sideways on - force attacker to the sides
- Jockey - touch tight away
- Make attacker move to beat you
- Time your challenge

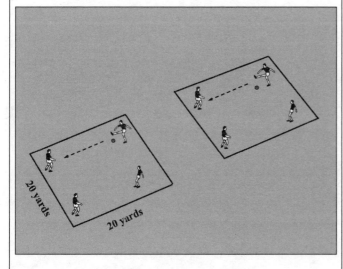

Organization - 2 v 2 Defending

In a 20 by 20 yard grid, X1's pass to either of X2's. X2's work together to try and dribble past X1's end line. X1's have to defend as a partnership - only moving to defend after X1's first touch. Award a point for every tackle.

Progression(s)

- Award points for attackers reaching end line
- Rotate pairs and partners to test players
- Bring in goal for attackers to shoot at
- Add in two goals at opposite end for defenders to pass through

Key Factors

- Nearest player closes the ball down
- Second player provides cover at right distance and position
- Defenders shape should work like a pendulum - nearest to the ball - the other covers
- Communication from back defender

Defending

Organization - Recovery Runs

Defenders play 3 v 2 in a 30 by 20 yard grid. Defender 3 loses possession to A1 by passing back to them. Attackers 1 and 2 have to try and dribble to one of the markers to score. D1 and D2 try to stop them as does D3 who makes recovery run to become balance defender.

Progression(s)

- Rotate players and positions
- Award 1 point for attackers scoring at halfway markers - 3 points for end line
- Take away markers and put in a goal at end
- Add an extra attacker
- Add a goalkeeper

Key Factors

- Individual defending as before
- Work on the defender D3 getting goal side and providing cover and balance for D1 and D2
- Use goalposts as marker for recovery run
- Communication between defenders is paramount

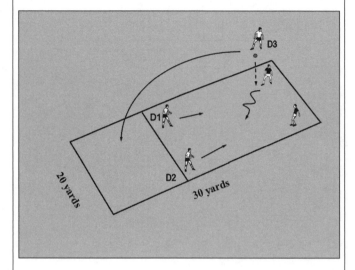

Organization

In a 20 by 40 yard grid four attackers play against 4 defenders. Defenders (D) start with the ball - pass it into attackers (A). All players must stay in zones. A's have to dribble ball over D's end line. After A's first touch D's can close down and defend.

Progression(s)

- When shape is there - remove zones
- Bring in a goal for A's to attack
- Bring in two goals for D's to pass out through - points for all goals
- Add in a goalkeeper for D's

Key Factors

- Work on the role of each defender - nearest player closes the ball - others provide cover, balance and depth
- Increase this to a half field practice - phase of play defense v attack
- Communication

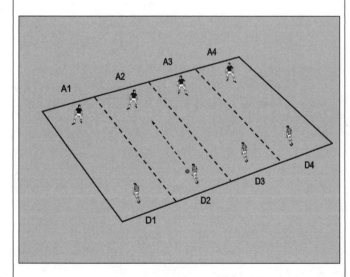

Defending

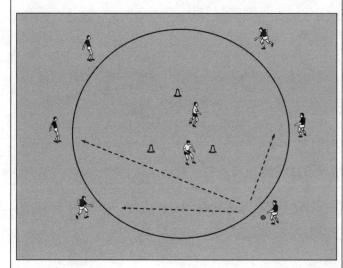

Organization - Blocking and Positioning
Attacking players line up around a 10 yard center circle with two defenders in the middle. Three central cones in a triangle indicating three goals. Players on the outside try and score through any of the goals.

Progression(s)
- Defenders have to stop ball going through the goals without using their hands
- Increase or decrease the goal size if certain players are struggling
- Limit players on the outside to two touch
- Rotate defenders every three minutes

Key Factors
- Communication - between two defenders
- Decision making - close down passes or guard goal
- Positioning - minimise the running by covering space cleverly
- Although a defending drill players on the outside should be passing quickly and taking lots of shots

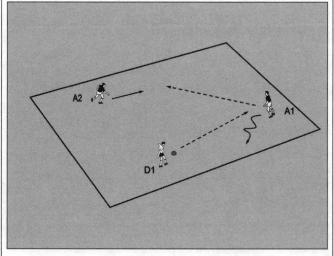

Organization - Decision Making
Defender D starts with a pass to X1. X1 and X2 have to attack and get ball over the end line. X2 starts beside D but becomes active after the first pass. Offside is in play.

Progression(s)
- Rotate positions after five attempts
- Introduce a small goal for D to defend against
- Increase goal size and add a goalkeeper
- Limit attackers time to score

Key Factors
- Decision making - can defender win the ball off X1's first touch? - if not how close to defend-cover?
- Stay on your feet - don't dive in
- Keep play in front of you
- Try to make attackers play predictable

Defending

Organization - Marking and Sweeping

Within a 20 by 40 yard field, play 5 v 5 including goalkeepers. One sweeper (S) in each end zone - three players each playing man for man in center zone. Players in center zone have to beat their marker and they can then go unopposed up against sweeper and goalkeeper.

Progression(s)

- No other players except for the one with the ball may go into end zones
- GK's must start every attack - supply of balls in each goal
- Allow the sweeper to advance if they win the ball back in the later stages of this game

Key Factors

- Man to man marking - be tight and frustrating
- Sweeper should be mirroring the play in front of them in the end zone and ready for the break at all times
- GK and sweeper should be communicating to the players in front of them
- Encourage inventive midfield play - i.e dribbling

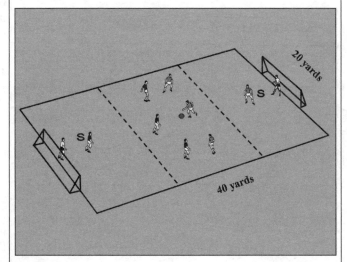

Organization - Directing Players

Two lines of players side by side. The players have to run to each marker in a zig zag formation over 40 yards. Before they get to each marker the coach will shout inside or outside.

Progression(s)

- Players treat each marker as an opponent and have to direct that player inside or outside as the coach requests
- As first pair reach second marker - the next players can begin
- After completing circuit players join end of line

Key Factors

- Quick sharp running to close down space
- Curve your run to the marker appropriately
- Form good, angled, low positions when you reach the markers
- React quickly to each command and return fast

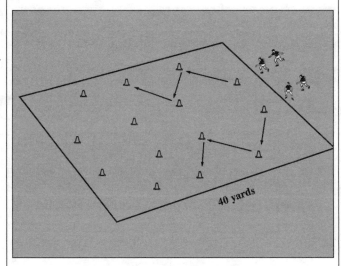

Defending

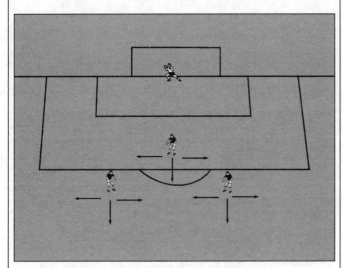

Organization - Communication - Team Shape
Start with your usual defensive formation and the goalkeeper playing on half field. The coach begins shouting commands up - push up - drop - drop back - left, right etc. Players have to take up realistic positions on the field to your commands.

Progression(s)
- Get the fullback, center back, sweeper to take over the shouting
- Bring in rest of defensive players - defending midfielders, wingbacks etc.
- Add commands like down - where they drop to the floor or head where all players jump up for a header etc.

Key Factors
- The importance of this drill is to establish commands that all the team recognizes and can follow - as well as finding who is the best communicator in defense
- Players must react quickly and coach them into good positions
- Defense must work together as a unit

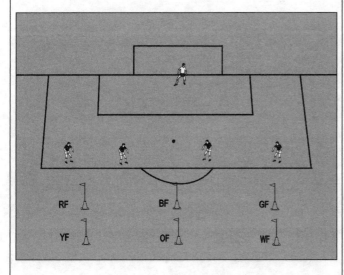

Organization - Team Shape
Set up as previous on half field with six different colored flags across the field as shown. Start with your normal defensive formation. Coach shout out a color flag and the players form the shape they would in a game if the ball was at that flag.

Progression(s)
- As players become used to taking up the correct defensive positions - change the flags positions
- Get a defender to shout the color of flag where the ball is supposed to be
- Introduce your midfield ahead of the defenders

Key Factors
- Players must react quickly to the call and get in position early
- Make sure adequate balance and cover is there at all times
- Players should after a while need little coaching
- All players should be communicating as they play and should be telling each other where to be

Defending

Organization - Pressuring The Ball

In a 20 by 30 yard grid four attackers line up facing four defenders. Very simply the attackers pass the ball side to side. The defenders have to communicate between them who is to pressures the ball.

Progression(s)

- Attackers do not come forward at first - rotate every position
- Once communication and closing down is fluid, add a goal behind defenders and let attackers move freely

Key Factors

- Communication is vital - all defenders talk constantly
- Nearest player pressures the ball
- Other players provide balance and cover as instructed
- Do not tackle, just keep play in front of you and as predictable as you can

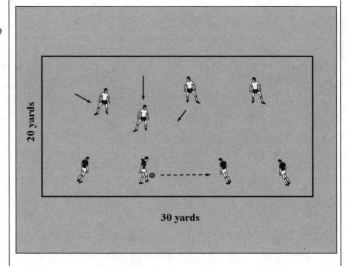

Organization - Defending From The Front

On a full half field play 7 v 7 with the defending team having a goalkeeper. Midfielder shoots at goal - GK plays out to defending team who try and pass out through to halfway line goals. Attacking team have to win ball back and attack the goal with the GK. Rotate plays in and out of each positions.

Progression(s)

- Condition the game as you need to
- Encourage the fact that you are trying to win the ball high up the field and restrict the defending team playing out
- limit players touches on the ball or condition O team to making at least five passes before scoring at center, etc.

Key Factors

- Anticipate the short throw out from the goalkeeper
- Split the defenders - give the keeper a dilemma
- Close down the receiving player quickly and force into playing where you want them to
- Attackers should work as a unit - pushing up together squeezing the play and forcing defensive errors

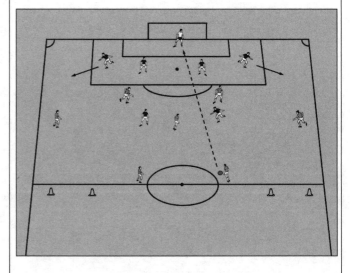

Tackling

Challenging for and winning the ball is a very large - very important part of the game and often correct techniques are not taught and practiced, here are a few key considerations on dealing with tackling:

- Players need to have a confident attitude - a desire to win the ball
- All tackles require good timing
- Decision making is a key factor in tackling - can you win that ball?
- Use your body weight to get power into the tackle
- Correct body positioning will allow for a better tackle - approach to the ball

Tackling can also involve a number of other things:
- Reading the game - interceptions - vision
- Tackling is a means to an end - and must keep possession after regaining it
- Tackles can be clearances averting dangerous situations
- Tackles can also be used to start attacks

Players should always be encouraged to stand on their feet and work on timing a challenge correctly however the sliding tackle if used in the last resort scenario and when taught correctly can be a valuable asset to a players abilities.

Types of tackles:
- Aerial tackles
- Block tackles
- Sliding tackles

Players can improve their physical strength but the best training is to work on their decision making and timing - players must go in 100% as this is such a physical part of football and if you do not you run the risk of being injured.

Tackling

Organization - The Block Tackle

In pairs players stand one feet apart with their left foot beside the ball each. Players both count to three and on "three" make a block tackle on the ball. Repeat five times with each foot and rotate partners.

Progression(s)

- Move players back one pace and repeat sequence
- Move players back three paces and repeat sequence

For all these drills players should move on the count of three and try to connect at the same time with the ball.

Key Factors

- Use inside of the foot to block with opponent
- Lean your shoulder and knee inwards for strength
- Connect at the same time and the ball should not move
- Plant the non kicking foot and generate power through the body into the ball

Organization - Timing and Forcing Possession

Similar set up as previous with X1 now dribbling slowly to X2. X2 moves towards X1 as they dribble and has to time the block tackle and force the ball over the challenge to get possession. X1 offers resistance.

Progression(s)

- Players tackle five times with each leg and rotate partners
- As timing of tackle gets better X1 should increase resistance
- Players must still connect with the ball at the same time and X2 forces the ball through after the initial block

Key Factors

- Bide your time and wait for the opportunity to block tackle
- As you block tackle, force your foot over the opponents and take the ball
- X1 should allow the opportunity to block
- Players must tackle with the nearest foot and plant non kicking foot early

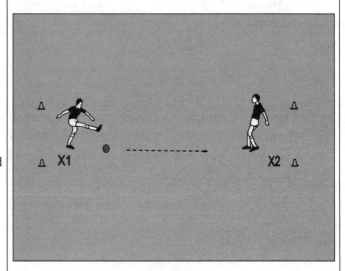

Tackling

Organization - The Slide Tackle

X1 starts five feet in front of X2 - X2 is slightly to the side. X1 dribbles slowly away from X2 so they can catch up. X2 comes in from an angle tackling with furthest foot to scoop ball away from X1.

Progression(s)
• Repeat five times from each side and rotate players
• When timing is there allow X1 to jog at half pace
• Allow X1 to play at full pace

Key Factors
• Players must realize the sliding tackle is a last option and needs to be a controlled slide and not a jump in
• Be patient
• Come in from an angle at the side - not directly behind
• Make the challenge - scoop technique and get up as quickly as possible

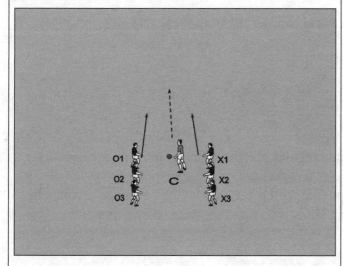

Organization - Winning The Ball

Players are paired up in two lines 15 yards from the coach. The coach plays the ball forward and at any time shouts go. Pairs compete to win ball and play a pass back to the coach.

Progression(s)
• Vary starting positions of players - lying down etc.
• Rotate partners frequently
• Change your position as coach after the pass so players have to look up before they find you
• Award points for passes

Key Factors
• Players must react quickly
• Use your body to get in front on opponent and shield the ball
• If second to the ball - make a quick decision look to slide or block tackle to stop the pass or try to get goal side - i.e. in front of coach

Goalkeeping

No other aspect of soccer demands anywhere near as much specialist training as the goalkeeper. Everything from the physical to the practical through to the psychological aspect of goalkeeping is unique compared to the rest of the squad. It is somewhat surprising then that in recreational and in youth soccer the needs of a GK are often over looked when training teams, yet when trained and developed properly this is the area that can have more influence over your team winning or losing a game than any other.

When training GK's there are many aspects to consider and many areas to cover.

- The ready position
- Handling
- Footwork
- Positioning
- Distribution
- Shot stopping
- Diving
- Dealing with crosses
- Organizing the defense
- Organizing set-plays defending
- Playing as a sweeper

There are areas that involve specific techniques that can be taught as above and also areas that come naturally and can be nurtured such as:

- Agility
- Anticipation and decision making
- Bravery

Although it is often easy to let the GK's join in a regular practice and assume they are benefiting from the small sided games or shooting practices, coaches are encouraged to incorporate GK specific skills in any practice they can - i.e. 'passing and receiving' let the keepers use hands to catch and throw - simple solutions to providing GK's with extra position specific practice.

Goalkeeping

Organization - Reflexes

Working in pairs. X1 stands in goal - with back to X2. X2 shouts turn and throws ball at goal. X1 has to spin and make reaction save

Progression(s)

• Both players act as GK
• Vary height and pace of throw
• Increase distance apart and shoot with feet

Key Factors

• GK's must be up on toes and in ready position
• X2 must shout then immediately release the ball
• Vary shots - make GK work on different saves
• Make the Save

Organization - Quick Reactions

Same set up as previous but now facing each other. X1 stands two feet in front of goal facing X2 who is three feet away. X2 rolls ball through X1's legs. X1 has to spin and make save - so ball does not cross line.

Progression(s)

• Both players act as goalkeeper
• Vary pace of roll
• Shoot with feet

Key Factors

• GK's must be up on toes and in ready position
• X2's passes must be of a sensible speed
• Make GK work - keep the passes coming
• Make the save by collapsing on the ball - protect rebounds

Goalkeeping

Organization

Working in threes. X1 stands in goal and X2 and X3 line up level with goalposts six yards from goal. X2 throws at goal - X1 saves and shuffles across goal to make low shot save from X3.

Progression(s)

- Servers must have a supply of balls
- X2 should try and hit top left corner and X3 should hit bottom right
- Increase pace of shots and time between shots to test GK's ability
- Allow for rebounds if GK is very good at saving
- Increase distance if serve is good enough

Key Factors

- Serves must be accurate
- Serves should give GK a chance to get there in time
- Really make the GK work
- GK's must save and bounce up quickly for next save
- Spring off nearest leg and save with nearest hand - keep strong wrist

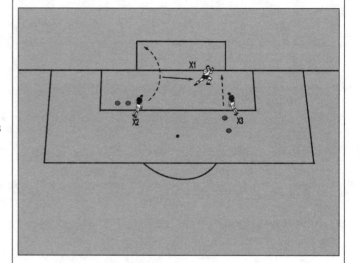

Organization - Last Minute Dives

Players form a line in front of the goal. Each player has a number. Coach shouts number and then strikes at goal. All GK's dive out the way except the number called.

Progression(s)

- Rotate formation of line
- Start with soft serves - move to full volley shot
- Increase distance between you and GK's

Key Factors

- Players should stand strong for shot
- Numbers not called - maintain a solid dive
- React quickly whatever
- Try and make a proper save
- React as a game situation

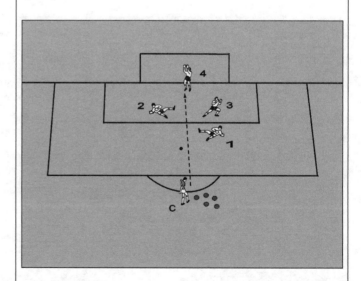

Goalkeeping

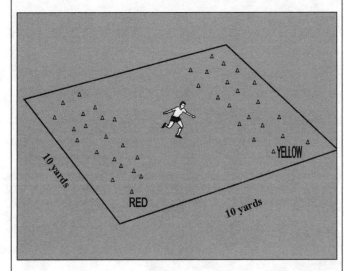

Organization - Warm Up Footwork
X stands in the middle of a 10 by 10 yard grid surrounded by yellow and red markers. X has to turn over as many alternate yellow then red markers in one minute.

Progression(s)
- Introduce more colors
- Every player to practice
- Reduce time of practice
- Compete two players against each other

Key Factors
- Players must shuffle sideways - click heels
- Keep low center of gravity
- Stay in ready position
- Spring out of stride after turning over marker
- Keep a steady pace

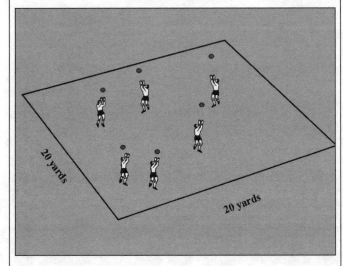

Organization - Jumping / Collapsing
Every player has a ball in a 20 by 20 yard grid. Players jog - side shuffle etc around. On coaches command players have to perform task set. (1) Collapse on ball (2) high catch.

Progression(s)
- Players throw ball up for themselves at first
- Players should exchange balls with someone else
- Vary height and pace of serves into other players

Key Factors
- Players must perform correct techniques
- Collapse with hands on ball and body protecting spillage's
- High catches - jump off one foot - knee up to protect yourself
- W - hand shape

Goalkeeping

Organization	Diagram

Organization - Quick Hands

Every player has a ball in a 20 by 20 yard grid. Players perform tasks set by coach.

- Bounce ball - clap hands and catch ball
- Bounce ball - clap twice and catch ball
- Bounce ball - Clap three times and catch ball

Progression(s)

- Increase number of claps to extortionate level!!!
- Bring in a spin after claps and still catch ball
- Bring in a spin and pose on one knee before catching ball

Key Factors

- Concentrate on the ball
- Clap quickly and keep eye on the ball
- On the spin - maintain balance and focus
- Enjoy the drill

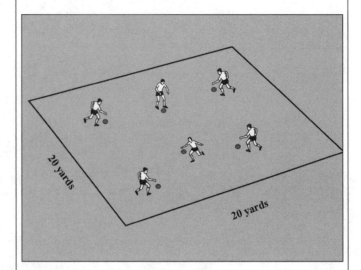

Organization - Upper Body Rotation

Working in pairs players stand back to back. X1 has ball in hands and turns to right and passes to X2. X2 rotates upper body from left to right and hands ball back to X1. Repeat.

Progression(s)

- Limit time and count passes completed
- Do over-under sequence. X1 through legs X2 over head etc
- Sit players toe to toe - make them sit up - pass, lay back - touch ball on ground over head - sit up, pass and repeat
- Do with feet - players lay head to head

Key Factors

- All drills to be performed at high pace
- Quick hands
- Full rotation of the body
- No throwing ball to catch breath - must be passed
- Maintain focus under pressure and when disorientated

Goalkeeping

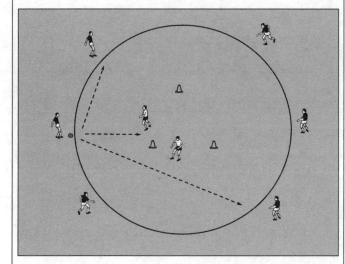

Organization - The Alamo!!!

Two goalkeepers in the center of a circle. Players on the outside pass the ball around and try to score through any of the three goals in the center triangle. Rotate the goalkeepers every three minutes

Progression(s)

- If GK's are very good allow them to play in the center on their own
- To speed shots up, play two touch on the outside or one touch if ability will allow

Key Factors

- GK's should be up on their toes and shuffling from side to side - heels clicking
- Enforce good diving technique and correct handling
- Try to catch shots and eliminate rebounds
- Communication between both GK's is vital

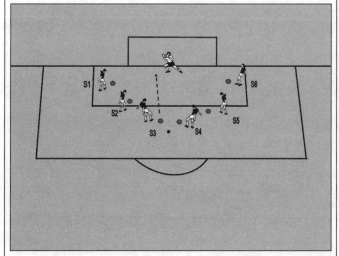

Organization

One goalkeeper and six servers with a supply of balls positioned around in a semi-circle five yards from the goal. Each server has a number and coach calls out one number at a time to strike the ball at goal to beat the GK.

Progression(s)

- Servers should vary height and pace of each shot at goal and give GK adequate time to get in position
- Once GK has got the quick footwork - move the servers back five yards and work on closing down the angle around the semi-circle

Key Factors

- Always be aware of your position in the goal
- React quickly to the number of server called and shuffle with quick feet across goal into saving position
- Hands should always be in ready position
- Handle each shot properly

Goalkeeping

Organization - The Complete Goalie Drill

One goalkeeper with five outfield positions with an equal number of players at each station. L starts by lobbing a throw high for the GK to call for and claim. GK then distributes out to opposite side O. O plays give and go with S and shoots at GK.

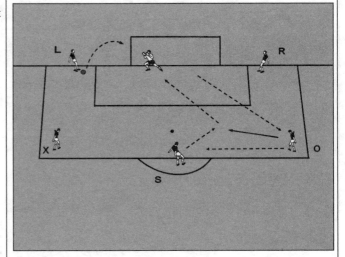

Progression(s)

- Repeat from opposite side with R starting and X finishing
- Players rotate one position in sequence each time i.e. L to O - O to S - S to L etc.
- Rotate GK as well
- Allow S to shoot or lay off to keep GK guessing

Key Factors

- Big shout for the ball - jump correctly and turn and distribute quickly with an overarm toss
- Get in position early for each stage and shuffle feet
- Close down at correct angle for shot and make appropriate save
- Be alert when S has option to shoot or lay off

Organization - Goalie Wars

Two teams of two GK's on a 30 by 15 yard game field with two full sized goals. Teams have to score past the opposition by kicking, throwing, punching the ball in the oppositions goal. Players must stay in their half of the field. First team to score three goals wins.

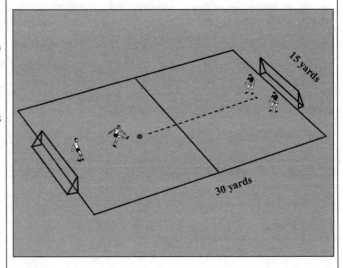

Progression(s)

- Play the game like a world cup competition where all teams get to play each other once
- Award two points for each victory
- Team with the most points are the winners of Goalie Wars

Key Factors

- This game should be fast and furious - each team trying to catch the other team out of position or not ready
- Teams decide whether to defend and attack side by side or one in front of the other
- Although for fun, correct-handling, shot stopping, throwing, punching, drop kicking should be adhered to throughout

Goalkeeping

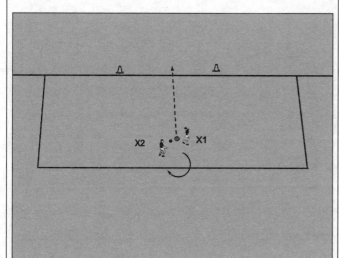

Organization - Goalkeeper Squash
Place two cones in front of a wall or use a kick back goal. One GK serves from the back line by throwing the ball at the goal. The second GK has to catch the ball before it hits the floor. Each GK takes it in turns to serve.

Progression(s)
- If the ball hits the ground the other player scores a point
- Allow GK's to use half-volleys or drop kicks
- Allow full volleys
- Combination of all techniques

Key Factors
- Try to throw/kick with power and at an angle
- React to the opponents throw/kick quickly and anticipate the deflection off the wall
- Catch and re-strike the ball as fast as you can to keep your opponent moving
- All correct techniques

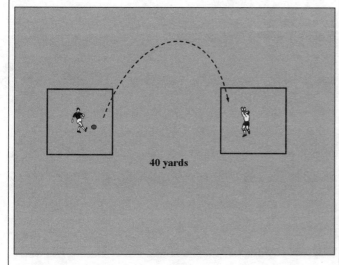

Organization - Drop Kicks
GK's in pairs stand in the center of their grids facing each other 40 yards apart. GK's try and score by drop-kicking the ball into the opponents grid. Players catch the ball and return it to opponents area.

Progression(s)
- If ball bounces in the grid - player scores two points - if from a full volley not a drop-kick one point
- If ball bounces outside of grid opponents get one point
- This can be a 2 v 2 game in larger grids or singular in four grids
- Rotate partners

Key Factors
- Strike ball on the laces as it hits the floor
- Follow toe through to target area
- Get under flight of ball and catch at highest point with hands in correct W position
- Try to catch opponent out quickly
- Vary height and speed of kicks

Goalkeeping

Organization - Quick Transition

Two goals are placed on a field two thirds normal size. O1 begins by crossing into area for the GK to come and claim. The GK calls and then claims the ball and immediately delivers up field for the two X's. The two X's go 2 v 2 against two O's and try to score past GK at opposite end of field. Play until a finish.

Progression(s)
- O1 should have a supply of balls - opposite end GK can practice distribution to O1 after finish
- This drill can be built up with crosses coming from both sides, add in attackers pressing the GK and then defenders and attackers, as you wish, to create more game-like situations

Key Factors
- Big positive claim to begin the drill
- Get head up before and after you catch and know who you are clearing it to
- Select appropriate clearance - long throw, drop-kick etc.
- Communicate to player and distribute quickly and more important, accurately

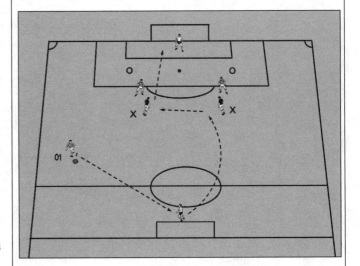

Organization - Goalkeeper Soccer

On a 25 by 40 yard game field two teams of equal number plus GK's. Normal scrimmage except the team in possession plays normal soccer and the defending team has to use GK techniques only i.e. diving, catching etc to win the ball back.

Progression(s)
- Rotate the actual GK position for each team
- Use larger or smaller field dimensions depending on age, ability and group size

Key Factors
- Encourage quick transition - players must switch mentalities when they lose possession
- Utilise being able to use your hands - stay up on feet and bide time to dive in for tackling
- Reinforce good technique in every aspect of play

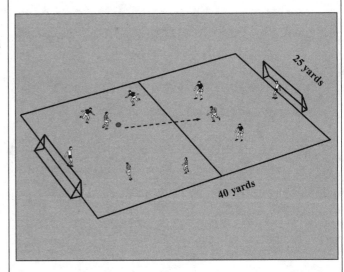

Games

Do you:

ALWAYS FINISH YOUR PRACTICE WITH A FIVE-A-SIDE?
ALWAYS LET THEM PLAY A SCRIMMAGE IF YOU'RE STRUGGLING FOR IDEAS?

It is a very easy option to let your players scrimmage off. Nine times out of ten this is the favorite part of a kids practice - the game at the end, but the real question is:

Are your players putting into practice all of the things you have just taught them in your coaching session?

There is a definite need for players to just play and have fun with limited instruction from the coach. The next section contains a few "games" that can be just as much fun as the scrimmage or are even slightly adapted scrimmages, that can not only be benefit the players enjoyment but their learning as well

Things to consider with 15 minutes left in your session:

• Can we place a condition on the players for the first five minutes that relates to today's practice? i.e. session - shooting - condition - one touch finishes only

• Can we play a game involving soccer skills that benefit each and every individual?

• Do these games allow everyone equal touches on the ball - equal playing time?

• What can we work on as a team in the scrimmages? i.e. one touch play

As a coach you decide what you think the team needs most, if they have worked hard and need to just play then that is great - let them. If you need to reinforce the skills and tactics you have been working on with them in training, then condition the scrimmage for the first five or ten minutes and make the players think a little while they are still having competitive fun.

Often the games can be used to give players a rest period with two teams playing and one team watching. Other times games can be used to work players harder by adding endurance elements to the practice or stacking one team against the other to work defenders or goalkeepers.

The beauty of coaching is that you have the freedom to structure any practice, any game, to get the most out of your players - and we don't always have to play 'a match'-'a scrimmage' just to keep the players happy at the end.

Game Play

Organization

Two teams of equal numbers play in a 30 by 20 yard field with goals placed at either end. There is a cone placed in opposite corners. Players stand on center on sidelines and wait for number to be called. X's compete against O's to score a goal after running around corner cone.

Progression(s)

- Introduce two balls
- Make players dribble ball around marker and then score - whilst stopping opponent at the same time
- Condition scoring foot
- Use two, three, four numbers at a time

Key Factors

- React quickly to number being called
- If first to the ball - shoot at earliest opportunity
- Take your opponent on
- When dribbling- reinforce technique and good shooting habits when in competition

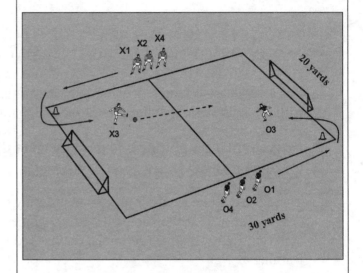

Organization

Two equal teams play in a 50 by 25 yard game field. There are four corner goals and 10 by 10 yard center square that no-one can enter. Each team defend the two goals at their end of the field. Point for each goal

Progression(s)

- Introduce two points for successfully switching the ball to a team mate through central zone
- Bring in one touch finish rule
- Condition players touches - two touch
- Introduce goalkeepers

Key Factors

- Aim is to keep possession and look to switch ball early to attack corners
- Communication and movement are vital as ever
- Look to capitalize on passing through neutral zone in the middle
- Take shooting opportunities early

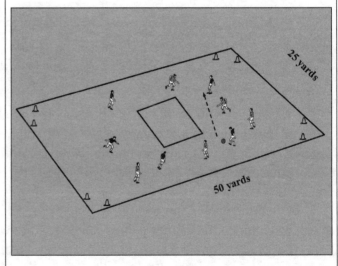

Game Play

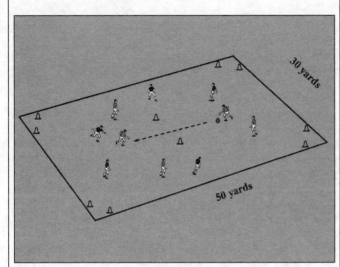

Organization
Same set up as previous with two equal teams playing now in a 50 by 30 yard game field. Center square is replaced with goal. Each team defend the two goals at their end of the field. One point for each goal and three points if you can score through center then end goal in same move.

Progression(s)
- Bring in condition that players must play through center goal to score
- Bring in one touch finish rule
- Condition players touches - two touch
- Introduce goalkeepers

Key Factors
- Get head up early and look to switch the play
- Draw defenders in with possession and counter attack opposite corner
- Look to create space for switched pass
- Avoid dribbling unless one on one
- Strike at earliest opportunity in front of goal

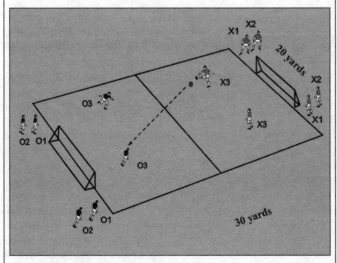

Organization
Four teams all numbered in corner of the game field. When numbers are called, players run to middle to compete against team at opposite ends two numbers

Progression(s)
- Award points for each goal scored
- Call more than one number
- Add GK's
- Replace goal with stand up cone - must hit to score a point
- One touch finishes only

Key Factors
- React quickly when number is called
- Work with team mate from adjacent corner
- Shoot early if chance is there
- Team with most points wins

Team Games

Organization - Long Ball

Two teams of equal numbers - batting team/fielding team.
Coach (C) - passes ball to first batter (B1) - they must kick
the ball and keep it on the field. Batter has to run to opposite
end and back - fielders (F) try to hit batter with the ball as
they run. Remaining batters stay off the field.

Rules

- Each batter who makes it there and back scores a point for
  their team
- No hands allowed for fielders - five points for opposition if
  they use them
- Fielders have to get all batting team out
- If batter kicks ball into the air - fielders get one header
  batter is out - two headers the whole team is out

Key Factors

- Batters: aim for spaces on the field - run zig-zag
- Fielders: keep ball moving - quick passes, only shoot at
  player if a team mate is behind the batter
- Everybody on the fielding team should be moving - no
  standing
- Batters should be numbered and bat in order
- Team with most points after two innings - wins

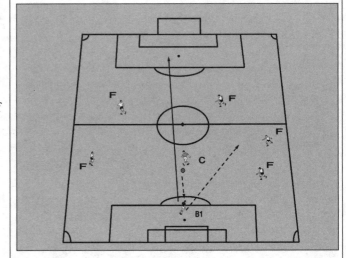

Organization - Football Golf

Five equal teams. A target is chosen and teams have to hit
target with least number of kicks. Players in each team take
turns in sequence.

Rules

- For each hole make a par for players to do the hole in
- Coach keeps score for all teams
- Vary height, distance and size of each target

Key Factors

- Use different range of strikes to aim for targets
- NO HANDS
- Every player must have a turn in each round
- Adjust par according to players abilities and ages

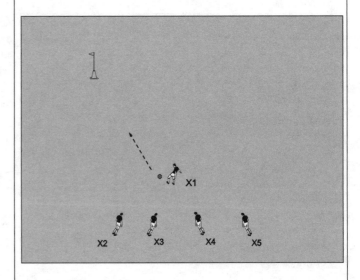

Team Games

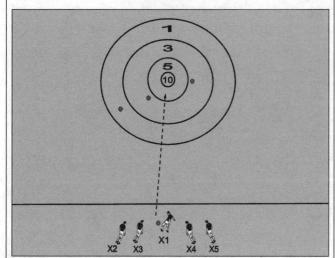

Organization - Football Bowls

Five equal teams. First player in each team tries to pass ball into marked circles. Teams go in sequence. After each round balls return and next player goes.

Rules

- Each team gets to go first in different rounds
- If ball finishes in:
  – outer circle - 1 point
  – second circle - 3 points
  – third circle - 5 points
  – inner circle - 10 points
- Other players can knock balls out of the way on their turn

Key Factors

- Try to weight your pass into the circles
- See if you can knock other balls out of the circle and keep yours in
- Team with most points wins
- Adjust passing distance according to age/ability

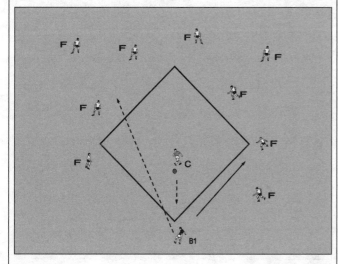

Organization - Football rounders/baseball

Two teams of equal numbers - batting/fielding teams. Coach (C) passes to first batter (B1). Batter must kick ball through diamond. Batter tries to run around the bases.

Rules

- Fielders (F) try to hit bases before batter gets there or hits batter while they run to bases
- If batter kicks ball in air - fielders get one header, batter is out - two headers the whole team is out
- No use of hands or five points to other team

Key Factors

- All fielders should be alert for headers or to run and get ball into bases quickly
- Batters should stay off field until their turn and must bat in sequence until whole team is out
- Team with the most runs after two innings - wins
- Coach should always bowl/pitch

Team Games

Organization - Non-Stop Football Cricket

Two teams - batting and fielding team. Batting team lines up and are numbered. Coach passes ball to first batter - they must kick the ball forward and run around marker to their left or right - batter keeps running around alternate markers until they choose to stop. They have to run for each ball bowled at them. Fielding team are spread across the field and have to get the ball back to the coach as fast as possible so the coach can then pass the ball and try and hit the marker in the middle before the batter runs back in time.

Rules
• If batter misses a pass they still have to run
• If the ball hits the center cone they are out
• If batter kicks ball in the air and fielders head the ball once
  - batter is out - if they head it twice - two separate players
  - the whole batting team is out

Key Factors
• One run awarded every time batter crosses middle cone having run around outside markers
• Both teams get two innings - whole team has to be out for innings to end

Organization - Football Cricket

Batting team (B) and fielding team (F) line up as shown in diagram with coach (C) bowling for both teams. Two batters at a time - bowler passes ball to wicket (cone) trying to hit it. Batter tries to kick ball as far as possible and swaps ends with fellow batter. Fielders try to hit cones at either end before batters run back to them or get it back to coach.

Rules
• Batters score a run each time they cross on the middle of cones which are 20 yards apart and get back to cone before ball hits it
• If batter kicks the ball and it goes beyond the boundary lines they score four and do not need to run - if it goes over the boundary lines without and bounces they score six and do not need to run
• If ball hits cone from coach or fielders before they run there batter is out

Key Factors
• Fielding team has to get all batters out until only one is left so they can not swap ends
• Bowler bowls to alternate ends after six bowls in one direction

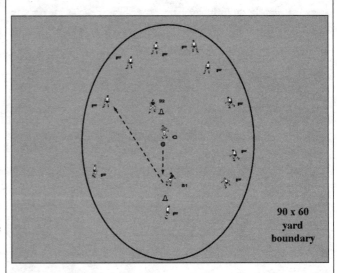

90 x 60
yard
boundary

Team Games

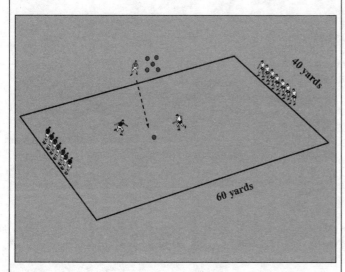

Organization - The Wall Game

Two equal teams with each player numbered stand at opposite ends of a 60 by 40 yard game field with arms linked together. The coach stands to the side in the middle with a supply of balls. Coach calls out a number and that number player from each end runs to the middle to compete. Players called out go one on one and have to try and score by chipping the ball over the heads of the "wall" of players at the other end - play continues until somebody scores.

Progression(s)

• If the players in the wall break the link - the other team is awarded a penalty kick - where they get a free chip from 10 or 15 yards - depending on age and ability levels

Key Factors

• Outfield players can play back to the wall at any time but players must not break their links
• After a few rounds the coach should call two or three or even four numbers at a time to compete

N.B.
All these games are for fun and useful alternatives to a scrimmage or five-a-sides, however the skills involved and techniques should be stopped and taught correctly if players are struggling with the games.

Game Play

Organization - Two balls Game!!!

Two teams of five compete on normal game field - one team rests. Coach begins the game and throws two balls into the air. The first team to score two goals wins and they stay on to face next team.

Progression(s)

- No team allowed to stay on for more than three matches
- Condition teams so that two different players must score the goals
- If one team is dominating condition them to two, or three touch play depending on ability

Key Factors

- This game heightens players awareness as they are keeping their eye on two balls at any one time
- Teams must decide to have certain players follow a certain ball or keep a general team shape and all play with both
- Organization and communication are the key to success

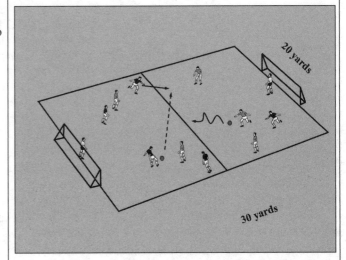

Organization - Man Adventure Game

The game begins 5 v 5 Attack (A) v Defense (D) plus a goalkeeper. Attackers have to try and score as many goals as they can, defenders clear the ball beyond half way line. The attackers start each attack from halfway. After one minute a defender is removed after two minutes a first attacker is removed.

Progression(s)

- Each minute there after a defender then an attacker are removed until after ten minutes of play there is only attacker against GK for one minute
- The defending team then swaps with the attacking team and the game begins with one attacker against GK for a minute - then a defender is added - players are added each minute alternately

Key Factors

- The game finishes after twenty minutes continuous play with 5 v 5
- The team with the most goals wins
- Fittest players should start for each team each round - this is a game of endurance and skill
- Make the ball do the work
- Use your man advantage - wear opposition down

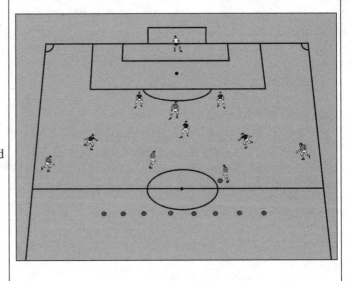

Game Play

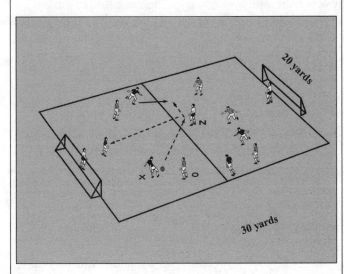

Organization - The Playmaker
Two goalkeepers, three teams and one playmaker (N). Two teams of five playing with one team resting. First team to score a gaol wins and stays on to face next opponents. Two touch play except for playmaker who plays for both teams.

Progression(s)
- Idea of game is to use the neutral playmaker to create goal scoring opportunities
- Bring in conditions that playmaker must assist all goals or make playmaker one touch only and work them harder
- Rotate the neutral playmaker role

Key Factors
- Neutral player must be always looking to support the player on the ball
- Teams should look for quick counters with or without N's help
- It is important the resting team should rest and get good recovery time while the other two teams play

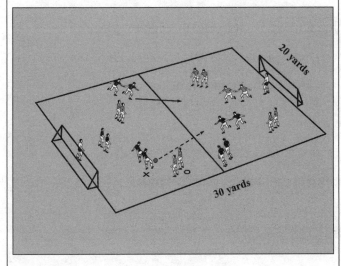

Organization - Three Legged Soccer
Two teams of equal numbers with every outfield player joined hands with a team mate - they must not at any time break hands. Normal soccer is played between the teams and the team with the most goals wins.

Progression(s)
- Award a penalty for any players breaking their link
- Link a partner to each GK as well so they have to save without breaking their link
- This game is for fun and to build team spirit but players should still try to perform to a high level

Key Factors
- Work with your partner
- Get in a rhythm for movement with and without the ball
- Communication is vital between each and every partnership as well as the entire team

Tactical Coaching

As you develop as a coach and as your team develops in age and ability - the need for technical coaching begins to decrease and the need for tactical coaching increases. Here are a few pointers when coaching tactics to your players.

Fail to Prepare - Prepare to Fail

You know your players and team better than anybody and know what they need to work on but you must know the topic - research for drills, have more than you think you need in case things don't work out as you think they will. The most fundamental factor when coaching anything is that you have to be prepared - know what you are teaching and you will be far more confident teaching it.

When working with young players remember to use this method

How?   **When?**   **Where?**

For example, creating space as a tactical session.

How?
• By running wide

When?
• As soon as you are sure the GK has possession and we want to attack/counter attack

Where?
• Provide the players with guidelines as to where to run - use cones if necessary

If you are working on GK's distribution to the defenders then:

How?
• By selecting appropriate technique - roll out - over arm toss - pitch technique

When?
• As early as possible once the 'free' player has created space

Where?
• Do you throw into space or into feet?

This "method" might just help you structure the learning environment for your young and they can be involved in this process by using careful question and answer.

Playing Out From The Back

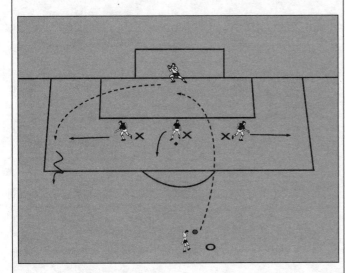

Organization
O plays ball into GK. X's create space to receive pass. GK throws out. X receives and runs ball out over end line.

Progression(s)
- Vary delivery positions - get goalkeeper to throw out in opposite direction where there is maybe a numerical or space advantage
- Once O plays ball to GK they can decide which X to close down and pressure
- Introduce a second O - leaving only one unmarked X player

Key Factors
- Create space quickly - spread out quickly
- Delivery from GK - to space or feet
- Receiving body position of X's - open to field of play
- Forward thinking/forward moving
- Positions of players without ball (supporting/covering)
- Communication between X's - can anyone get out?

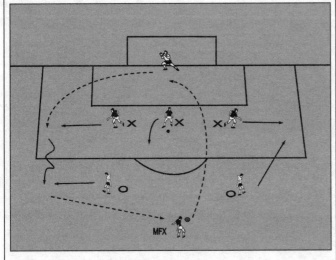

Organization
Ball is played into GK. Two O's close down X's. GK throws to 'free' X. Can X in possession find a MFX with the ball? X's then support midfielder behind the end line.

Progression(s)
- Bring in a player to close down MF's when in possession
- Bring in two MF's and play against one O after end line
  - the one O closes one MF down and the X's have to find free MF with ball

Key Factors
- Work on MF's position to receive ball from X's
- Movement of X's once MF's receives the ball should be just in advance of MF or just behind
- Work on combination plays between X's and MF's against new O's

Playing Out From The Back

Organization

Continuation of previous exercises with extended playing area. Ball played into GK and X's spread the field to received pass. Reward points for successful play outs from GK's through defenders to MF's.

Progression(s)

- Bring in a striker for MF to find with ball
- Add in defender to mark Striker X

Key Factors

- Concentrate on MF's runs to support other MF's when they receive the pass from the ball - should leave a pass to a defending X on to support and then play out again
- Angles of support by X's to MF's - don't watch pass - support the play

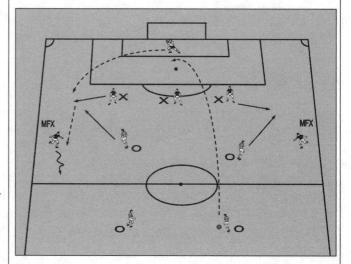

Organization

Repeat drill above now with Striker for X team. The object is to get ball from GK to SX. Reward points for successful play outs.

Progression(s)

- Let O's attack the GK and X's
- Bring in more defending O's and more attacking MF and SX's
- Allow to play normal 8 v 8

Key Factors

- If MF's split, then SX should show short for pass from X's
- MF's should pull inside with diagonal runs to create space down flanks for SX
- X should look to spin short then receive past defending O's into space

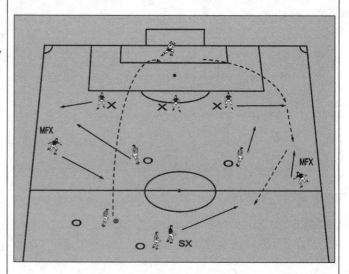

Transitional Play & Counter Attacking

Diagram	Organization

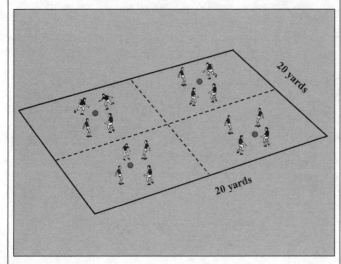

Organization
Four players in four 10 by 10 yard grids. Players throw ball between them in number sequence. On coaches whistle, ball transfers one grid clockwise and repeat.

Progression(s)
- Players use feet
- Players play one touch if possible
- Players use driven pass when transferring ball to next grid

Key Factors
- Body shape
- Communication
- Movement
- Quality of passes - weight and accuracy
- Control on long reception

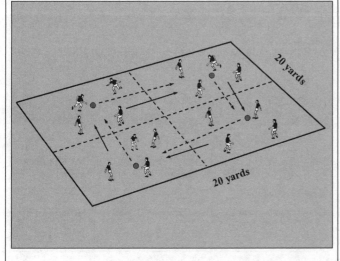

Organization
Same set up as previous. On whistle, player passes clockwise then supports pass by moving to that grid. Players no longer have to pass in number sequence.

Progression(s)
- After first support runner introduce second support runner
- Bring in a third runner so only one stays then make all transfer
- Last player should control long pass then support team mates in grid

Key Factors
- Curve your run to next group
- Each player to make different support run
- Try to play one touch on control into support runners and continue one touch where possible

Organization	Diagram

Organization

Using just over half field. T1 plays ball into midfield area 30 by 30 yards where there is a 4 v 4 situation. Teams play keep ball and can use either of wide T's to help their team.

Progression(s)

- On coaches whistle the O's try and dribble out of area and find O9 or O10 with the ball
- This creates a 3 v 2 going to goal - play until a finish
- Create 4 v 2 with two support runs and then add a defender - creating a 4 v 3 to goal

Key Factors

- Quick reaction to whistle - use space ahead of them
- Angles and support of forwards O9 and O10 as well as midfield O's supporting them
- Quick interchanges - try to get behind X's
- Speed and communication

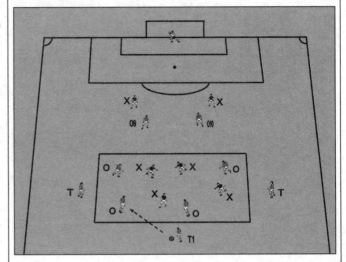

Organization

S1 plays ball into O2 who controls and plays ball into O4 - as ball is passed X2 can make recovery run creating a 5 v 4 situation. O's attack X and play until a finish. Repeat from opposite side with S2 passing to X3.

Progression(s)

- O2 and O3's work in pairs and rotate with players behind them each round
- Let defenders and attackers switch roles after ten minutes
- Make X's play out through center goal
- Change S1 and S2 as O7 and O8 and have them join in attack. X2 starts now by marking up against O4.

Key Factors

- Encourage being comfortable in possession
- Wide player's should "open up" when receiving passes so that they can see the 'forward' option
- Support play - in advance and behind
- Decisions - speed of attack - point of attack
- Create space

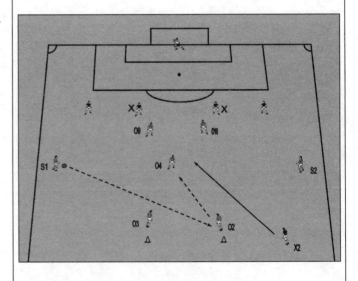

Attacking In The Final Third

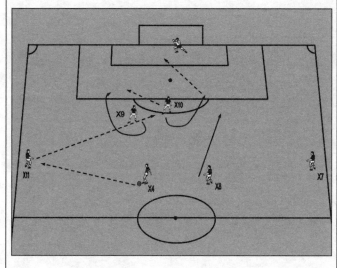

Organization

X4 passes to X11 who receives and runs with ball and passes to X9. X9 moves in line with pass and lets run for X10. X9 spins out but X10 can play, pass or shoot. Repeat on both sides.

Progression(s)

• Rotate players in and out of positions
• Place touch restrictions on all or certain players if speed of drill is not there
• X9 now spins inside and offers
• Introduce X8 making a deep run to support X10

Key Factors

• Pace and accuracy of the pass - hard and driven
• First striker creates space
• Communication from second striker - "over"
• Support from other players
• Technique of shot/cross
• Timing of late run

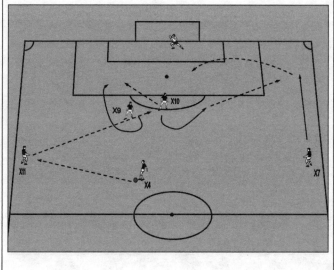

Organization

Same set up as previous (without X8). X10 now turns, X9 now pulls away for an angled pass from X10 or X10 plays ball forward to X7 who has overlapped.

Progression(s)

• Repeat both sides
• Rotate all players in
• Play one touch where possible

Key Factors

• Pace and accuracy of the pass - hard and driven
• First striker creates space
• Communication from second striker - "over"
• Support from other players - timing of movement/runs

Attacking In The Final Third

Organization

X4 passes to X7. X7 passes to X9 and follows the pass. X9 passes back to X7. X10 spins out for pass from X7. X9 and X8 make forward runs to finish from X10's cross.

Progression(s)

- Repeat from both sides
- Rotate players in
- Play one touch where possible

Key Factors

- Technique of shot/cross
- Pass and accuracy of the pass - hard and driven
- First striker creates space
- Quality of layoff and the weight and accuracy of the through-ball
- Support of other players - timing of movement/runs

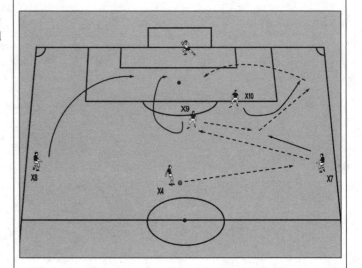

Organization

X8 passes to X7. X7 passes to X9 and follows, X9 passes back to X7. X7 switches to X4 who breaks forward to shoot.

Progression(s)

- As with all other drills use both sides of the field and rotate players - in each drill if very successful you can add in a defender - passive at first or two defenders then make them active

Key Factors

- Technique of shot/cross
- All exercises should be done quickly and sharply, fast movement - quick passes - good communication and varied movement. Encourage players to be creative and make things happen - even if planned

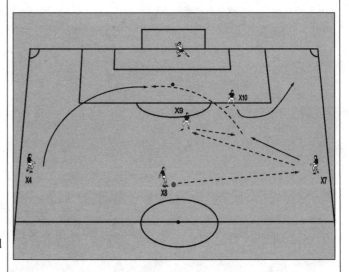

Developing Young Players

Diagram	Organization

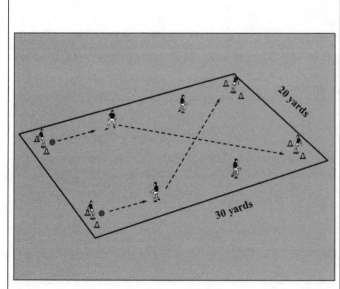

Organization
Within a 20 by 20 yard grid, two teams of eight players, one team inside the grid and the other outside. O's throw the ball into X's who receive and throw out to another O on opposite side of that square. Two minutes and rotate players. Repeat the drill with feet.

Progression(s)
- After players receive correctly with hands and feet, remove central lines and allow players to pass off to any outside player not just the one opposite.
- Encourage two touch play if possible
- Add cones in center area for players to dribble through
- Remove cones and add two defenders to pressure ball carriers

Key Factors
- Receive sideways on
- Receive with furthest foot and play across body with opposite foot
- Keep body shape open
- Keep head up and know next pass as ball arrives
- Lots of communication and varied movement to create good passing angles
- Quick sharp footwork between cones

Organization
Four corner goals of five foot width with a player in each. X's in bottom goals pass to central players who receive on half turn and play diagonally across to far end goals - repeat from both sides several times and rotate players.

Progression(s)
- Add in defenders to mark central players - always have two balls going at the same time
- Get players in goals to overlap after making initial pass to center
- Center players play one two and then send to opposite corner where goaltender has had to return quickly

Key Factors
- Open up to receive and play in two touches
- Use body to protect from defenders in the turn
- Quality of passes - weight, accuracy length
- Overlapping and movement should be sharp and passes one touch on give and go's
- Quick spins off defenders
- Lots of communication

Developing Young Players

Organization
Same set up as previous now with center goals instead of corners. Ball starts with GK's who play into central regions - play out to one of two wide players - who play or cross in for finishes. No tackling in wide zones.

Progression(s)
- If passing sequences are failing make team not in possession passive and increase their tackling privileges as quality improves
- Players should still look to play two touch when receiving and one touch from the outsides - one touch finishes

Key Factors
- Look for quick release to the flanks
- Players should look to support early and make runs into dangerous areas for the crosses
- 5 v 5 in smaller area so every player should be able to receive at all times from all positions

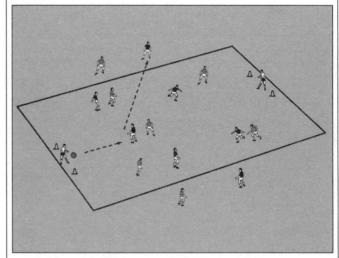

Organization
On a full sized field, GK throws to X1 who plays in for X2 - plays back out for X1. X1 plays back inside for X3 who plays out for X4 who plays one-two with X5 and delivers cross for X5 and X6 to finish.

Progression(s)
- At exactly the same time O's are working same passing sequence in opposite direction
- When movement and passing is fluid bring in passive then active defenders in the central zones - then out wide
- Keep both balls playing

Key Factors
- Quality passing
- Quick incisive movement
- Communication
- Support as individuals and team
- Good forward runs from wide - sharp attacking runs into danger areas
- One or two touch play
- Need end product
- Mobility and recovery runs

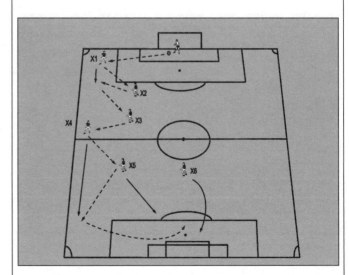

Diagram	Organization

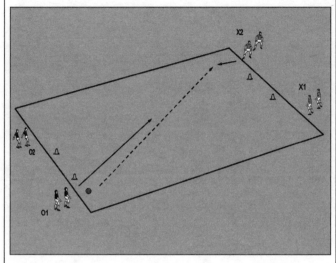

Organization
O1 plays the ball to X2 who tries to score at opposite end. O1 closes down X2 and tries to win ball back - players swap lines. O2 repeats drill form their side against X1. Add a goalkeeper.

Progression(s)
- Repeat last drills but now O2 becomes covering defender for O1
- They are now playing two defenders against one attacker
- At first O2 is only allowed to communicate - no actual defending - then allow defending

Key Factors
- Close down quickly - force outside - be patient - win the ball
- Covering defender should be constantly talking - show inside - show outside
- Covering defender must win ball if first defender is beaten

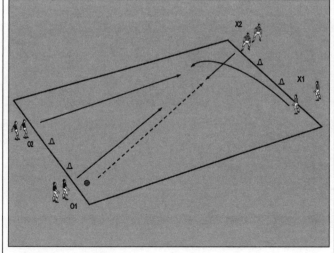

Organization
Same set up as before but now progressed to 2 v 2. After X2 receives pass from O1 - X1 makes overlapping run to support attack. O2 as the nearest defender closes the ball and O1 makes decisions, communicates to cover and balance.

Progression(s)
- Players rotate ends after each attack
- Progress to adding extra sweeping defender - at first only allow communication - then allow to defend fully as 2 v 3
- Bring in third attacker to create 3 v 3

Key Factors
- Communication
- Decision Making
- Discipline
- Maintain shape - compact
- Do not ball watch
- Close down - deny space
- Force into predictable play
- Provide cover and balance
- Patience: to win ball - then keep possession

Defending Creativity

Organization

Two lines of attackers X. X1 plays into coach and spins out to create wide option for X2. Coach plays ball back to X2 who plays out side for wide run from X1 who crosses. X2 attacks the cross. O's defend and clear.

Progression(s)

- Rotate attackers lines
- Repeat from left and right sides
- Replace coach with third attacker who attacks the cross as well
- Introduce a fullback to pressure the crosses
- Add second wide player attacking from deep and fullback to defend them

Key Factors

- Communication and verbal support from central defender to partner, then fullbacks
- Maintain shape when a back four - always provide cover and balance
- Try to clear forwards - do not give up corners - maintain possession if possible

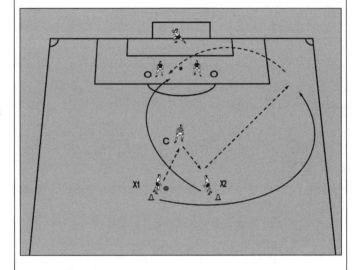

Organization

Following on from previous progressions create a 4 v 4 from 40 yards out. X1 or X2 starts the move and try to incorporate inventive attacking play to unbalance the defense and get behind and score.

Progression(s)

- Bring in two target players for the attackers and play 6 v 4
- Add a defensive midfielder - then a second creating a 6 v 6
- When defenders become comfortable, change shape of attack - play three out and out attackers, three midfielders and two attacking defenders against them - add two wide defending players to create 8 v 8

Key Factors

- The defense must work as a unit - maintaining solid shape and not being drawn out by the creativity and movement of attackers
- Defenders should not drop too deep or pressure too high - denying space in behind them, the GK can act as a sweeper covering central players
- For all these drills attackers and defenders should rotate and play in each others roles

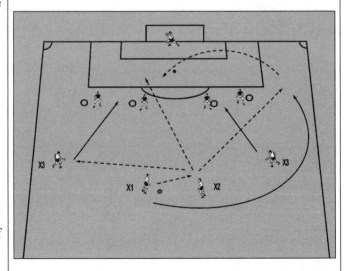

Cool Downs

The Importance of Cooling Down

- All athletes should take time to cool down after practices and games:
  - To maintain well being and fitness levels
  - To avoid aching and stiffness

- They can be done with our without a ball and should last at least 10 minutes

- Players produce waste product in the form of lactic acid during exercise which remains in the system - this needs to be worked out of the body

Components of a cool down
- Light exercise that brings the heart rate down
- Stretching that last a minimum of 30 seconds per muscle
- Fluid retention - helping provide vital hydration
- A small snack to help replenish vital carbohydrates used during practice

Considerations
- Stretching when the muscles are warm will increase flexibility and elasticity
- Fatigue and its effects may not be felt right away but cool downs should still take place immediately after activities
- Cool downs can provide teams time to reflect on performances
- Encourage players to cool down as a team
- This can be an enjoyable experience

ALSO AVAILABLE

VOLUME TWO

This book of coaching sessions follows on from the technical drills and exercises laid out in Volume One and progresses to the technical aspects of the game in functional situations,
as well as dealing with the tactical development of young players. It should act as a useful reference tool for you to use and adapt to your own coaching style as well as provide a few fresh ideas you might implement with your players.

Some of these drills you may have seen variations of and may have used before, others will be new to you. They have been collated from the author's (Rob Gale's) playing and coaching experiences with Score UK/ The Fulham Academy. Other drills have been adapted from many experienced and talented coaches who Gale has had the pleasure to work with over the years in various other English Youth Academies.

You will notice there is not age or skill guidelines placed on any of the drills; this is because only you as the coach will know your team's ability levels and their knowledge and skill. It is your job as the coach to determine what your team deficiencies are and hopefully this book will help you confront those issues and break down ways into which develop your young players to a higher level – the professional level.

No doubt over time you will be able to adapt or change ideas or sessions to suit your own style of practice and indeed the needs of your players or squads. The beauty of coaching is that there is no right or wrong answer and the test for us as a coach is to try to make our players become the very best they can be. I hope you enjoy the step up in difficulty of these drills from Volume One and good luck implementing them.

www.scoreuk.com

"Setting the standards others can only imitate and strive to achieve"

OVER 20 YEARS OF INTERNATIONAL COACHING EXPERIENCE

QUALIFIED, PROFESSIONAL, EXPERIENCED STAFF

TAILOR MADE CAMPS OR TRAINING PROGRAMS TO SUIT YOUR CLUBS NEEDS

(NO FORMULAIC ROUTINE CAMPS LIKE THE BIG COMPANIES REGURGITATE EACH YEAR)

SPEAK TO US AND SEE WHY WE ARE ONE OF THE FASTEST GROWING COACHING COMPANIES IN NORTH AMERICA

WE OFFER PROFESSIONAL PRODUCTS WITH PROFESSIONAL STAFF

PLUS WE ARE - THE ONLY INDEPENDENT CAMP COMPANY WITH DIRECTS LINKS TO AN EPL CLUB

DO YOU WANT TO TAKE YOUR TEAM/CLUB/ REGION TO THE NEXT LEVEL?

ALWAYS WANTED THE CHANCE TO PUT YOUR PLAYERS INTO A PROFESSIONAL ACADEMY WITH A CLEAR ROUTE TO COLLEGE OR PROFESSIONAL SOCCER HERE AND ABROAD?

THE SCORE UK SOCCER FULHAM ACADEMY

SCORE UK SOCCER IN ASSOCIATION WITH FULHAM FOOTBALL CLUB ALREADY RUN AND OPERATE THREE FULL TIME PROFESSIONAL SOCCER ACADEMIES IN NORTH AMERICA. PLAYERS STILL STAY WITH THEIR CLUB TEAMS BUT GET INDEPENDENT, DISCIPLINED, STRUCTURED TRAINING FROM OUR PROFESSIONAL CURRICULUM - WHICH BENEFITS THEM, THEIR CLUBS, THEIR COACHES AND OFFERS THEM A CHANCE TO SHOW CASE THEIR TALENTS TO THE WORLD – NO OTHER COMPANY CAN OFFER ALL THIS.

TEL: 402 504 1718 – OR - 402 884 5309 – WWW.SCOREUK.COM

TALENT IS NOTHING WITHOUT OPPORTUNITY

BOOKS

$24.95

Item # 1011
This is the most comprehensive book ever written about the 4 - 4 - 2 formation. Covered are the roles and responsibilities of the defenders, midfielders and forwards in both attacking and defending situations.

BEST SELLER!

$29.95

Item # 1001
The most comprehensive book EVER published of soccer practices and training sessions. **Over 200 pages** full of training sessions from **Manchester United, Brazil National Team, PSV Eindhoven, Boca Juniors**, etc.

1,000's ALREADY SOLD!

$29.95

Item # 1014
Over 100 training sessions from the world's top teams like **Manchester United**, Ajax, **Liverpool, Juventus, PSV Eindhoven and São Paulo**. These, plus sessions from National teams from **Holland, Italy, USA** and others make this book a "must have" for any serious soccer coach.

$19.95

Item # 1007
This one-of-a-kind book shows every training session, practice and drill of the Penn State soccer team from their 2001 season where they reached the NCAA Tournament round of 16.

$24.95

Item # 1013
This incredible book shows every GOALKEEPER training session, practice and drill done by the New England Revolution from their 2002 season.

$19.95

Item # 1009
A great NEW book by **Anson Dorrance**. *Vision of a Champion* is a unique blend of technical advice and powerful inspiration that gives youth players, parents and coaches the secrets of over 25 years of success developed as a collegiate (University of North Carolina) and U.S. National Team coach.

$12.95 **$12.95** **$12.95** **$12.95**

All Four Books

$39.95

Item # 1002, 1003, 1004, 1005 - All four books # 1006
These excellent books contain material from the 2000 and 2001 issues of the WORLD CLASS COACHING magazine. Each book includes training sessions from the world's top teams like **Manchester United, Liverpool F.C., Juventus F.C., Ajax F.C., PSV Eindhoven, São Paulo** plus many of the **MLS teams**. Each training session includes a detailed explanation and is accompanied with easy-to-read diagrams.

$14.95

Item # 1010
This book is perfect for both the knowledgeable and inexperienced/ parent coaches of 9 - 12 year old teams.

Included are 32 complete training sessions covering **passing, receiving, dribbling, running with the ball, shooting, defending and goalkeeping**. There are also 16 fun, small-sided games that can be used in any training session or as warm-ups.

$14.95

Item # 1008
This book is perfect for both the knowledgeable and inexperienced/ parent coaches of young teams.

Included are 32 complete training sessions covering **passing, receiving, dribbling, running with the ball, shooting, defending and goalkeeping**. There are also 22 fun, small-sided games that can be used in any training session or as warm-ups.

To Order Call
1-888-342-6224

OR VISIT

WORLDCLASSCOACHING.COM

DVD's

International Coaching Three-DVD Series
Featuring Coaches of
Manchester United - Liverpool F.C. - Leeds United

$34.95

$34.95

$34.95

TACTICS and DRILLS for PASSING and POSSESSION

TACTICS and DRILLS for ZONAL DEFENDING

TACTICS and DRILLS for ATTACKING and GOALSCORING

Item # 4001 - Attacking
Item # 4002 - Defending

Item # 4003 - Possession
Item # 4004 - All Three DVD's

Buy All Three DVD's For Only $89.95

TOPICS INCLUDE

Defending With a Flat Back Four

Zonal Defending

Improving Confidence For Heading

Developing Techniques For Youth Players

Developing Quick Play Using Circle Practices

Passing Progressions

Counter Attacking With Pace

Improve Your Shooting and Finishing

Build-Up Play For Crosses

Attacking In Waves

To order videos visit our web site

4-4-2 DVD's

$34.95

$34.95

Coaching the English Premier League 4-4-2 DEFENDING
By David Williams

Coaching the English Premier League 4-4-2 ATTACKING
By David Williams

Buy Both DVD's For Only $49.95

Item # 4005 - Attacking
Item # 4006 - Defending
Item # 4007 - Both DVD's

The 4 – 4 – 2 is the preferred formation for just about every team in the English Premier League. The 4 – 4 – 2 is also used by the majority of the world's top coaches and teams such as European giants Juventus, Real Madrid, Bayern Munich as well as the national teams of Brazil, England, USA, Italy, etc.

These DVD's will explain how the 4 – 4 – 2 formation is played, why it is so successful and why it is the formation of choice for the world's top teams. Coach David Williams (former Leeds United, Everton and Manchester United U19 coach) explains the roles and responsibilities of the defenders, midfielders and forwards, both in attacking and defending situations. The DVD's show many practices that he has used during his vast coaching experience in the English Premier League, and will show you how to train your players to play using the 4 – 4 – 2 formation. These practices start with 2 v 2 exercises and build all the way up to 11 v 11 conditioned games.

To Order Call
1-888-342-6224

OR VISIT

WORLDCLASSCOACHING.COM

BOOKS & VIDEOS

Item # 1008

This book is perfect for both the knowledgeable and inexperienced/ parent coaches of young teams.

Included are 32 complete training sessions covering **passing; receiving; dribbling; running with the ball; shooting; defending and goalkeeping**. There are also 22 fun small-sided games that can be used in any training session or as warm-ups.

$14.95

Item # 1010

This book is perfect for both the knowledgeable and inexperienced/ parent coaches of 9 - 12 year old teams.

Included are 32 complete training sessions covering **passing; receiving; dribbling; running with the ball; shooting; defending and goalkeeping**. There are also 16 fun small-sided games that can be used in any training session or as warm-ups.

$14.95

Item # 1001

The most comprehensive book EVER published of soccer practices, drills and training sessions. **Every page** is full of detailed observations of the training sessions of teams like **Manchester United, Brazil National Team, PSV Eindhoven, Boca Juniors,** and many of the **MLS teams**. All include easy-to-read diagrams of each practice.

$29.95

THOUSANDS ALREADY SOLD!

Item # 1009

A great NEW book by **Anson Dorrance**. *Vision of a Champion* is a unique blend of technical advice and powerful inspiration that gives youth players, parents and coaches the secrets of over 25 years of success, developed as a collegiate (University of North Carolina) and U.S. National Team coach.

$19.95

$12.95 **$12.95** **$12.95** **$12.95**

$39.95

All Four Books

Item # 1002, 1003, 1004, 1005 - All four books # 1006

These excellent books contain material from the 2000 and 2001 year issues of the WORLD CLASS COACHING magazine. Each book includes training sessions from the world's top teams like **Manchester United, Liverpool F.C., Juventus F.C., Ajax F.C., PSV Eindhoven, São Paulo** plus many of the **MLS teams**. Each training session includes a detailed explanation and is accompanied with easy-to-read diagrams.

Three-Tape International Coaching Series
Featuring Coaches of
Manchester United - Liverpool F.C. - Leeds United

Item # 2001, 2002, 2003 - All three tapes # 2004

In June, 2000 at Connecticut College, WORLD CLASS COACHING assembled on American soil for the first time ever, coaches from England's top Premier League teams, Manchester United and Liverpool F.C. for its International Coaching Seminar.

David Williams, Manchester United U19 Youth Team Coach and Sammy Lee, Liverpool F.C. Assistant Manager were joined by former Leeds United Coach, Mick Hennigan in this once-in-a-lifetime seminar. This three-tape series covers every session conducted by the three clinicians.

$34.95 **$34.95** **$34.95**

$89.95

All Three Tapes

To Order Call
1-888-342-6224

OR VISIT

WORLDCLASSCOACHING.COM